The BIG REDHEAD BOOK

Inside the Secret Society of Red Hair

St. Martin's Griffin
New York

THE BIG REDHEAD BOOK

ERIN LA ROSA

THE BIG REDHEAD BOOK. Copyright © 2017 by Erin La Rosa. All rights reserved. Printed in China. For information, address St. Martin's Press, 175 Fifth Avenue, New York, N.Y. 10010.

www.stmartins.com

Designed by Susan Walsh

The Library of Congress Cataloging-in-Publication Data is available upon request.

ISBN 978-1-250-11052-7 (hardcover)
ISBN 978-1-250-11053-4 (ebook)

Our books may be purchased in bulk for promotional, educational, or business use. Please contact your local bookseller or the Macmillan Corporate and Premium Sales Department at 1-800-221-7945, extension 5442, or by e-mail at MacmillanSpecialMarkets@macmillan.com.

First Edition: August 2017

10 9 8 7 6 5 4 3 2 1

TO MY PARENTS: *I OWE YOU FOR THE RED HAIR.*

TO MY BROTHER: *I'M GLAD YOU DON'T DYE YOUR HAIR BLOND ANYMORE, IT'S BETTER RED.*

TO MY HUSBAND: *I LOVE YOUR GINGER BEARD AND AM SO GLAD YOU LOVE ME FOR MY GINGER HAIR.*

TO MY FELLOW REDS: *LET'S BE FRIENDS?!*

CONTENTS

The **BIG**
REDHEAD
BOOK

Welcome, Fellow Reds and Red Enthusiasts!

L et's just get a few things out of the way: I'm not a stepchild, I don't have a fiery temper, and it's truly none of your business if my carpet matches the drapes. I know it can be confusing. Because those are things that seem to be openly and excitedly discussed when the topic of red hair pops up. But that's exactly why I'm here— to set the record straight. Like the undeniable truth that redheads have the hotter British prince. And that, much like ice cream, red hair is our greatest natural resource and needs to be protected at all costs.

Whether you have red hair or just like to admire nice things, you've probably noticed that redheads are virtually everywhere at this point—carrying a bow and arrow in Disney movies,* winning Academy Awards,† and singing

---

* Merida.

† Actress Julianne Moore for Best Actress in *Still Alice*.

duets with Taylor Swift on the radio.* It's like, what do these gingers think they are, special or something? (Spoiler alert: they are.) And even though they're seemingly everywhere and nowhere at once, like superheroes, the questions remain: What do we *really* know about them? Like, is it true they're going extinct? Or that they all came from Ireland? And do they hold redhead coven meetings? Because, ya know, they're witches…right?

It's only natural to have questions about gingers, especially if you are one. We look different than everyone else—that hair-the-color-of-a-sunset thing—and because of that people sometimes think we're different in other ways. Like you may have heard the vicious rumor brunettes† started that we don't have souls. Or that if you kiss us on Saint Patrick's Day it's good luck. And it's hard to know what to believe anymore—our eyes are naturally drawn to the fiery embrace of red hair, and yet society gives us mixed messages about what it means to be ginger (some good, some less so).

As a natural redhead, I want to answer your questions. In fact, I'm going to be wonderfully honest about why having red hair puts you in a class all your own. So here's the truth: we're pretty much the unicorns of the human world. Think about it: we're rare (only 2 percent of the world's population), beautiful (hello, Jessica Chastain), and have the ability to fly (see any of the Weasley family in *Harry Potter*). And because we're magical unicorns, we have a lot of secrets too; things that only redheads know to be true…until now.

Whether you have a tinge of ginge, know a redhead, or are just a run-of-the-mill red enthusiast, you've come to the right place. Welcome! I'll be serving as your guide into the realm of all things ginger. You're getting exclusive access into one of the most elite societies in the world—on par with Adele's squad

---

* "Everything Has Changed," by Ed Sheeran and Tay.
† By brunettes, I of course mean the creators of *South Park*, Matt Stone and Trey Parker.

and the Illuminati. And I'm going to let you in on all the top-secret things that only redheads understand. From why redheads actually smell different (and arguably better) than everyone else to how to raise a little redhead of your own, this book grants you a look inside our mysterious lives.

If you're a redhead yourself, then I know you have questions. Like, why do people always assume ginger women are sex kittens? And is it just you, or does going to the dentist seem like the most terrifying thing? I've got answers to those pressing matters and so much more. It's my job to remind you on each and every page that your red hair is a gift that goes way beyond hair color. By the end of this book you'll understand all the reasons why and feel empowered to share that gift with the rest of the world. (You're welcome.) But don't worry, my fellow reds: just because I'm sharing our most classified intel doesn't mean it cheapens anything we have. Nothing can touch the specialness of our ginger locks. And even if people know the ins and outs of being red, it doesn't mean they can ever fully *be* red. For instance, only redheads know the unspoken way we acknowledge fellow reds in public. It's like a superpower! You know what I'm talking about—that thing where you see another redhead out in the wild and give them a little nod of encouragement, a smile, curtsy, or tap dance. I think our ginger queen, Julianne Moore, explained it best when she said, "We redheads are a minority, we tend to notice each other, you know, and notice our identity." Let's go ahead and call this the "Gingers Unite" sighting. **#GingersUnite**

And like so many formative experiences, my first sighting happened in middle school during a summer theater camp. On that day, I stumbled into the black-box theater and adjusted my stirrup pants, slicked my tongue across my shiny metal braces, and scanned the crowd for an empty chair. Which is when I saw Katie, a fellow ginger. She and I locked eyes and that's when it happened—my first Gingers Unite sighting. Sure, I'd seen redheads before, and my brother had red hair too, but this was different. When I looked at Katie, she and I had a moment of recognition. It was like we both knew that no matter what, we had each other's backs. We were in this together, because we were cut from the same crimson cloth. She understood what it was like to be teased just because of hair color, the same way that I knew the horror of complete strangers trying to touch my hair. We accepted each other. And it was one of the most powerful and true feelings of my life.

There you have it, norms—which is what I'll call non-redheads from here on out—now you know what's happening when one redhead spots another. We have a connection. It's just one of the many hot tips I'll be sharing. And while a norm can never experience what it actually means to be a real redhead and sense that unspoken camaraderie, I'll give you the tools to soak up everything ginger. Because it's these little details that make redheads stand out in the world. And we are all over the world—not just in Ireland, as you may have been led to believe—because redheads aren't defined by one ethnicity: you'll find redheads from Brazil to Norway to Ghana, and all the points in between. We're different, and that's not just OK—it's amazing.

If it seems like I totally drank the red Kool-Aid and only believe in reds ruling the earth, that's only partially true. I had a sip, and want to share my drink with you all so we can go into this book experience with clear eyes and full redhead hearts so we can't lose. And I'm not trying to make the norms feel bad about their lack of ginger hair. I'm not. Being born without red hair isn't the end of the world. It's regrettable, but not the worst-case scenario. Being born norm just means it's important to educate yourself about redhead culture. For example, you may not know that only redheads can call other reds, "ginger." Otherwise, it's totally offensive and not a word we take kindly to.

REDHEAD SECRET:
Don't call us "Ginger" unless you are a ginger.

You also may not know that when you call us firecrotch, it automatically lands you on our list of people to casually forget about forever. So instead of continuing on in the world, unintentionally offending reds, take the knowledge I'm giving you in this book and put it to good use! Make a redhead friend, date a redhead, or buy a redhead a whiskey the next time you see one out. (Contrary to what you may have heard, we're not vampires . . . well, probably not.)

Being a redhead is a bonus in life. It makes you part of something singularly awesome, and that should be celebrated not just by gingers but by norms too. In this book we'll learn that being ginger affects not only your hair color but also every part of your life and how you live it. So let's grab life by the ginger roots and own the fact that reds will likely inherit the earth. Not just because our bodies make vitamin D better than other people, which I'll get into more later, but because it's becoming clear how important our existence really is. So go ahead, read on (or "red" on, if you prefer). It's the only way to fully understand that having red hair makes you one of the luckiest people in the world.

Congrats, my fellow gingers!

one

Pop CultuRED

Film, TV, and Redhead Stereotypes

L et me hold your hand, draw a bubble bath, and softly whisper in your
ear that redheads are the unsung kings and queens of the pop culture
world. Admit it: it's not just the jasmine bath salts talking; you agree that
redheads leave a lasting impression. Our red hair is like a life raft in the pop
culture sea of blond, black, and brunette hair—you can't help but doggy paddle
toward us! And indeed, you've definitely seen plenty of redheads on TV and
in movies. In fact, you're probably thinking of a specific one right now, aren't
ya? Bonus points if it isn't Wendy from the hamburger commercials. And it's
not just you; a 2014 report by Upstream Analysis found that 30 percent of the
TV commercials that run during primetime feature a redhead prominently.
During their research they even found that at one point, CBS showcased a
ginger every 106 seconds. That's a lot of red when you remember we're just 2
percent of the world's population. You get so much of the same on a regular
basis, that to see something different makes us instantly memorable—which
is probably just one of the reasons why advertisers are so keen to use us. As a
result, we've quietly infiltrated your viewing landscape, and now your bubble
bath. So, let's talk about exactly how this all came to be.

THE SIX KINDS OF REDS

For better or worse, pop culture is how most of us shape our identity. We see a character or view the world through a protagonist's eyes and we think to ourselves, *this person is exactly like me.* You may even start to emulate them, because you feel a connection you didn't know possible. Before you know it, you've joined Potterworld, inked a Gryffindor tattoo on your lower back, and booked your honeymoon to the Wizarding World of Harry Potter. So, yeah, pop culture is something that definitely defines us. And redheads are no different.

The only difference is that even though there are a lot of redheads in pop culture, they don't tend to be particularly diverse kinds of characters. I don't need to tell you that lack of representation is not limited to one group and certainly doesn't just happen to redheads. But because this is a book about redheads, they're who we'll be focusing on here. And while most other hair colors have an assortment of role models—the kooky brunette, the poetic brunette, the intellectual brunette, etc.—redheads have a much smaller pool to deal with.

For example, when I was growing up in a magical, roll-on-glitter-filled time called the '90s, the redheads I saw on-screen were people like Ginger from the Spice Girls, Scully from *The X-Files*, Amber from *Clueless*, Peggy from *Married with Children*, and Angela Chase in *My So-Called Life*. Only two of those people were my age, and none of them was a *natural* redhead. My brother, also a ginger, had an even smaller number of male reds: both Petes from *Pete and Pete*, and Budnick from *Salute Your Shorts*. That's three people my brother could emulate, and one of them (Budnick) was a bully. Needless to say, options for role models were slim. Redheads were there, but it was impossible not to sense the stereotypes people had from the roles you saw redheads in. A lot of these stereotypes still exist, and sometimes stereotypes aren't all bad. The real problem is that even if you don't fit the box people put you in, you have no control over how someone else will perceive you. But the best way to get rid of a harmful stereotype is to try and understand where it came from. Because when you do that, you can discern the fact from the fiction, and grasp that #notallredheads are one and the same. So let's grab a shovel and dig into the most prevalent depictions of reds in pop culture.

1. The Redheaded Vixen

Ah, the redheaded vixen. While all redheads are sexy motherfuckers who are too good for this earth, the vixen is something else entirely. Let's paint a visual: she walks into a room; her hair is loose, and her outfit is so tight it might actually just be her skin covered in paint. Chances are, she's after your man! So hide your kids and hide your significant other, because here comes this stereotype. And plenty of gorgeous red-haired women who are only after one thing have popped up on-screen: just remember Julia Roberts as Vivian in *Pretty Woman*, Julie Cooper (Melinda Clarke) from *The O.C.*, or Kate Mara as Zoe Barnes in *House of Cards*, to name a few.

DEFINITION: A sultry temptress with flowing red hair and curves for days.

KEY VIXENS IN POP CULTURE:

Joan from *Mad Men*, Satine in *Moulin Rouge*, and Jessica Rabbit in general.

So what's the harm in portraying women with red hair as sexual? Couldn't that be a good thing? Let's explore!

HOW IT HAPPENED:

From a psychological standpoint it's not hard to see why redheads have been sexualized in pop culture—red is the color of passion, and studies have shown that just seeing the color red can make your pulse increase.[1] It's inarguably the sexiest shade of lipstick. And while a little black dress is timeless, it's the little red dress you wear to feel smoldering. So, yeah, the color red is admittedly hot. And for ginger ladies, that just so happens to be our hair color.

STARE INTO THE CIRCLE.

IS YOUR HEART BEATING FASTER?

But how did this stereotype manifest in pop culture? Was it simply one redhead appearing on a screen and, BOOM, she changed our worlds forever? Not quite, because before there was even a TV or movie screen to broadcast our likeness, there was art. And redheaded women have historically been viewed as objects of desire in the art world. For example, let's take a look at a religious figure (in the Jewish tradition) who's often painted as a ginger on canvas: the evil demon Lilith. It's thought that Lilith was Adam's original wife, before Eve, but she decided to leave Adam because they were a terrible match. (Fun fact: the Lilith Fair music festival is named after her and her desire for freedom.) The mythology surrounding her has taken many forms, including her association with the power of seduction—she's been blamed for causing wet dreams by enticing

> *It is observed that the red-haired of both sexes are more libidinous and mischievous than the rest, whom yet they much exceed in strength and activity.*
>
> GULLIVER'S TRAVELS
> *BY JONATHAN SWIFT*

men in their sleep, for example. That sexuality naturally took form in art, a great illustration of that being the painting *Lilith* (1892), by John Collier. We see Lilith with a serpent wrapped around her like, well, a lover, or a snake she's just very oddly close to. But more important is her hair, which falls like a red blanket around her. It's alluring, suggestive, sultry, and plenty of other words that all translate to her being depicted as a ginger vixen. And it doesn't matter whether Lilith was actually a redhead because the viewer assumes she was based on what they're seeing.

So when you're examining how the vixen pyramid was built, you'll see our depictions in the art world close to the bottom, and Rita Hayworth somewhere in the middle. That's because the modern image of the redhead sexpot took off with Hayworth. Iconic Hayworth, with her gorgeous red hair (though she was naturally a brunette), really cemented herself into the pop culture world with her role in *Gilda*, where she played a femme fatale. In fact, her performance was so memorable that atomic bombs being tested during that time were nicknamed Gilda, after her bombshell character (much to Hayworth's disgust). But nonetheless, Hayworth was the first modern ginger temptress (though obviously not the last).

John Collier, via Wikimedia Commons, *Lilith*

OUR POP CULTURE PERSONA:
Hayworth made way for characters like Ginger in *Gilligan's Island*, Amber in *Boogie Nights*, and Ginger from the Spice Girls (apparently all vixen redheads are named Ginger). And it's still an image we see in the current landscape—looking at you, Melisandre from *Game of Thrones* and Olive in *Easy A*.

The vixen may not be overtly sexual at all times—who has that much energy?—but is often the focus of everyone's lust.

Indulge me, if you will, by examining Mary Jane in the *Spider-Man* series, or Tony Stark's affection for his flame-haired assistant, Pepper Potts. These two women aren't your stereotypical vixens, but they tempt our heroes and, in that way, become an object of longing and a version of the vixen redhead. There's also *Doctor Who*, a show where every Doctor since David Tennant has been obsessed with redheads and red hair. It's become a running joke, so much so that it led to this bit of dialogue in the series: "Loves a redhead, our naughty Doctor. Has he told you about Elizabeth I? Well, she thought she was the first."

Women in general are sexualized on a daily basis. That's a fact that we must shake our fist at the patriarchy for. But for redheads, it's a little more severe. It's similar to the way blondes have been stereotyped to the point where people sometimes joke that they're ditzy just by looking at them. With redheads, though, people assume we're going to pull out crazy shit in bed, like Michelle from *American Pie* did. Or if we aren't crazy in bed, we'll act crazy about sex, like Gloria in *Wedding Crashers*. It's not a coincidence that those characters have red hair. They cast redheads because, as a viewer, you know what seeing red hair translates to: you're in for a wild time.

WHAT IT MEANS FOR REDHEADS:

This stereotype doesn't just end on-screen; it bleeds into a redhead's everyday life. Like, say, one minute you're at a bar, having a drink with someone you think might actually be a sensible, normal person, and the next thing you know they've said, "I hear redheads are crazy in bed." You'd respond, except for the fact that you're sort of choking on the ice cube you just accidentally swallowed in shock. Now, to be fair, some redheads may lean into this stereotype—

Hannah: "She's such a slut in such a big way."
Elijah: "In a huge way. She used to do this thing where she would literally just rip the condom off."
Hannah: "Fucking redheads. Seriously."
Elijah: "I know, redheads, right?"

GIRLS

HOW TO RESPOND TO IT

When someone inquires after what you're like in bed, respond with any of these freebies:

1. "Yeah, I am great in bed. But now you'll never know because you asked me that dumb question."
2. "You know what they say: red on the head, I'll set fire to your bed if you don't back away slowly."
3. "This feels like the beginning of a really great excuse for me to leave this bar. BYE."

after all, sex is fun, and what's the harm in having another person know you're down for fun? But it's also legit to say that not all redheads want to be objectified that way by norms. So bottom line: think before you talk to us.

2. The Comic-Relief Redhead

Let's not beat around the fiery bush: gingers, on average, are funnier than everyone else. Maybe it's because we've been the butt of so many jokes that we've learned how to tell them, or that we're just genetically predisposed to have beautiful hair *and* magnetic storytelling skills. But the truth remains: people assume we might be funny when they see us, and there's a historical reason for this (other than our outstanding sense of humor).

DEFINITION: This redhead would be voted class clown, and they tend to be self-deprecating goofballs.

KEY GINGER LOLS IN POP CULTURE: Lucille Ball, Kathy Griffin, Conan O'Brien, and Louis C.K., to name a few.

HOW IT HAPPENED:

According to Professor Andrew Stott, who teaches the history of comedy at the University of Buffalo, we first began to see the circus clown as we know it—face paint and brightly colored wigs—in the early nineteenth century. The wigs needed to be bright to be seen from the backs of large theaters, and it's not hard to guess which bright but natural color was often chosen to take center stage in those performances. Professor Stott also speculates that the red-haired clown really solidified in our culture during the early twentieth century as a nod to the influx of Irish immigrants to America. That's right, my fellow Irish-American reds, it's entirely possible that we had a bit to do with this. Modern clowning tradition often plays on the juxtaposition of the clown as a rustic fool (in this case, the Irish immigrant is that fool) versus some savvy cosmopolitan element (e.g., the Irish living in big cities like New York). And Professor Stott went even further, telling me, "It's no accident, I would argue, that the Irish-surnamed Emmet Kelly was a (often red-haired) hobo clown, or that Ronald McDonald spells his surname the Irish way instead of the Scottish."

So it's fair to speculate that modern clowns, like Bozo, are influenced by the various historical depictions of the rustic fool. Which also explains why so many clowns choose to don a red wig. Whether they realize where these associations come from is another question entirely. But the role of the clown or the fool slowly developed onstage, making way for redheads to take control of the stereotype and shape their role as comics—like Lucille Ball's character in *I Love Lucy*, which is a kookier and arguably more charming version of the rustic fool, or Carol Burnett in *Annie* as Miss Hannigan, more of a drunken fool. So we've thankfully turned a corner and become comedians without the need for a rubber nose as well.

OUR POP CULTURE PERSONA:

If life teaches you anything, it should be that Lucille Ball was and always will be one of the funniest people this world has ever known. And while *I Love Lucy* may have aired more than fifty years ago (from 1951–57), Ball remains one of the most iconic redheads. A lot of people now know she was a natural brunette and not a real redhead, but it wasn't until she dyed her hair that she truly found success in Hollywood. The show aired in black and white but, even so, the viewer could almost sense her red hair shining through the muted tones on the screen. So she's an honorary ginger for that! Plus, she gave us this legendary quote to live by: "Once in his life every man is entitled to fall madly in love with a gorgeous redhead." Couldn't agree more.

The same year that *I Love Lucy* debuted, a show called *The Red Skelton*

Conan O'Brien ✔
@ConanOBrien

I asked nicely, but the DMV won't change the hair color on my driver's license to "pumpkin spice."

Show premiered, starring Red Skelton. He got his nickname from his hair and began his career as a clown and in vaudeville, eventually moving into film and TV full-time. Let's just say the '50s were a bit of a golden age for redhead comics.

And ever since Lucille Ball came onto our screens, many other funny redheads have tried to emulate her, like Grace on *Will & Grace* and Lily Aldrin on *How I Met Your Mother*. Comedians like Louis C.K. and Kathy Griffin are the hilarious stars of their own shows, while plenty of other reds, like Alan Tudyk, Maria Thayer, and Carrot Top (for better or worse), regularly get comedic sidekick roles.

WHAT IT MEANS FOR REDHEADS

If you already have a great sense of humor, the comedic redhead stereotype means that you're more likely to jump in when funny moments happen. When you know that people expect you to laugh things off, it's easier to joke about something. And if you have the license to be outrageous, it gives your personality room to grow and you can stop worrying so much about what other people think. In a lot of ways, this stereotype can be a huge advantage and explains why so many of us are incredibly charming.

That said, some would argue that our reputation for humor also puts redheads at a disadvantage. This is more so for men, since the traditional roles

Julie Klausner ✔
@julieklausner

2 ways I can tell if a guy won't be into me: 1) He prefers Mary Ann to Ginger 2) He is Hitler

in film and TV for ginger men are that of funny sidekick. Just look at Mitchell Pritchett on *Modern Family*—his relationship with his husband, Cam, is played on-screen more as a friendship than as a romantic partnership.

Or Noah Werner on *Suburgatory*, whose wife divorced him because she preferred her career to their relationship and whose housekeeper rejects him when he tries to start something with her. These examples suggest that if you're a male and a redhead in the comedy world, there's something slightly asexual about you. In fact, Conan O'Brien made a great joke about this phenomenon when he said, "A new study claims that red-headed women are sexually desirable but redheaded men are not. I wouldn't have minded, but the study mentioned me by name."

The reality is that the only way to combat this is to make roles for ginger men where they can display their comedic prowess and their sexuality too. Because there's truly nothing as sexy as someone who can make you laugh, especially if that someone is a ginger. Am I right, ladies?!

HOW TO RESPOND TO IT

When someone expects you to laugh something off, feel free to use these:

1. "I think I left my funny bone in the same place where you left your dignity."
2. "It's just hard to be funny under the strain of all my natural beauty."
3. "I'd totally make a joke, but I have to go fill my mouth with this glass of wine."

3. The Fiery Redhead

Are you sitting down? I hope you're sitting, because we're about to dissect the fiery-redhead trope and it might get a little . . . intense in here. It refers (primarily) to ginger women who are passionate, driven by their emotions, and unafraid to tell you when they're feeling those feels. A fiery redhead will have a large personality, and if you piss her off, well, you're going to know it. She may very well exhibit any of the following behaviors: punching, swearing, spitting, taking up a lot of space, and giving casual "fuck you" eyes. Fiery redheads can be totally ruthless, throw tantrums, and be charmingly candid. Which isn't inherently offensive—we're the feisty redhead and we're not going to take shit from anyone. As a result, some reds embrace this image or may blame their anger on that fiery temper. (Raise your hand if you've used that excuse before, my fellow reds.)

DEFINITION: Run for cover, because here comes a real no-nonsense kind of redhead. Quick to anger and always the one with the witty comeback, you don't want to get on this redhead's bad side.

KEY SPITFIRES IN POP CULTURE: Donna Paulsen from *Suits*, Ginny Weasley in the *Harry Potter* series, and Lydia Martin on *Teen Wolf.*

But the real question is: does the trope make the redhead fiery, or are all redheads the embodiment of that trope? Because if someone believes you're outspoken and won't take no for an answer, aren't you going to, on some level, play that part when you need to? And if you do get angry, because you're a normal human being, wouldn't it be easier to blame that on your hair? Let's find out!

> *She's a grown woman, a witch, and a redhead. You couldn't have stopped her if you tried.*
>
> ABBIE,
> SLEEPY HOLLOW

HOW IT HAPPENED:

If you like hearing about badass bosses who aren't afraid to go after what they want, then let's talk about the Viking age: a period lasting between the AD 790s through 1066. In our modern culture, the Vikings have been romanticized quite a bit, particularly with characters like Thor and a whole show on the History Channel called *Vikings*. And while the Vikings weren't quite the nonstop savage barbarians they are often rumored to be, they certainly weren't afraid to invade a territory and make it theirs. Many Vikings also happened to have red hair, which some believe is a direct cause of why red hair is so prevalent in Scotland, since it was along the Vikings' trading route.[2] So we have a group of people known for their ginger locks who refuse to take no for an answer . . . See where I'm going here?

Meanwhile over in England, after the Vikings, came William II (a.k.a. Rufus the Red) who reigned from AD 1087–1100. Whether he earned the nickname Rufus the Red as a result of his hair or his temper is up for debate. But in a 1930 satire of the English government, titled *1066 and All That*, William is categorized thus: "William Rufus was always very angry and red

> *I don't care much for redheads. Terrible tempers. But somehow it seems to suit you.*
>
> JAMES BOND,
> DIAMONDS ARE FOREVER

in the face and was therefore unpopular, so that his death was a Good Thing."[3] So even though this was a satire and undoubtedly tongue in cheek, clearly his fiery reputation stuck with him.

It's not just our historical ancestors who have brought about the stereotype, though, it's also perceptions of the color red itself. Red is traditionally thought of as the color of anger. Like, when we get angry, a common phrase you'll hear is that someone is "seeing red," and many of us say we turn "red in the face" when our anger boils up (we may also literally turn red). It's also a red flag that gets waved at the bull to get him riled up, and not a white one. So psychologically, red is a loaded color when it comes to temper and likely influenced the world's perception of our hair.

OUR POP CULTURE PERSONA:

The fiery redhead is so abundant in pop culture that if you ever hear someone say they can't think of an example, they are straight-up liars and you should feel free to call them that. Just look at Angela Chase in *My So-Called Life,* who, much to the dismay of her parents, became increasingly rebellious only after she dyed her hair red in the pilot. Or Rose in *Titanic*—she learns to spit like a man, refuses to listen to her mother, and ends the movie by running away with the man *she's* chosen. That's a tigress, if I've ever seen one. And Addison Montgomery on *Grey's Anatomy* and then *Private Practice*—she's confident, take-charge, and uncompromising when it comes to her work.

Fiery redheads also pop up in the more supernatural spheres of pop culture, like Jean Grey in the X-Men series. She has long flowing hair and is a superhero almost entirely ruled by empathy—she recognizes her telepathic powers after absorbing the emotions of a friend who died in her arms. In later comic books, she can use her Phoenix Force to create actual flames. Then there's the wonderfully obstinate Ygritte from *Game of Thrones*. She's "kissed by fire" because of her hair color, and she has absolutely no problem telling Jon Snow what's what—her most memorable line perhaps being, "Don't ever betray me, or I'll cut your pretty cock off and wear it around me neck." Pretty strong wording there, right? Those are just some of what we see on-screen, and it's a trope that likely won't go away quietly (typical fiery redhead).

> *You'd find it easier to be bad than good if you had red hair. People who haven't red hair don't know what trouble is.*
>
> ANNE,
> ANNE OF GREEN GABLES

WHAT IT MEANS FOR REDHEADS

When I was a freshman in high school, on my first day of English class, I was poring over the edition of *Great Expectations* we'd read that summer when the teacher, apropos of nothing, announced, "I know not to make you angry. I dated a redhead once and, woah boy, did she have a temper." Now, that put me in an odd position. Should I have poured out the gasoline in my bag and set fire to the place, or kept quiet so as not to prove him right? But more important: did my teacher actually think I was an angry person after ten minutes in his classroom? I'll tell you this: I hadn't been angry before he told me that, but all of a sudden I could feel the flames creep up the sides of my face. No one, and especially not an anxiety-riddled teenager, should have to go into situations where people already assume they know the kind of person you are based on how you look.

So you can see how tropes like the fiery-redhead one can have negative impacts in the real world. It's certainly less harmful than a lot of other stereotypes, but it does set up expectations for every redhead to fulfill. And, quite frankly, it's not easy to be fiery. Only some reds truly have earned that title, and it's unfair to usurp their powers in the name of a stereotype.

HOW TO RESPOND TO IT

When someone tries to suggest you're kissed by fire, put out the flames with these:

1. "Every time you call a redhead fiery, we get one step closer to world domination."
2. "I wanna do bad things to you, like stab you with this fork."
3. "The police still don't know what happened to the last person who called me crazy..."

4. The Evil Ginger

We assume a lot about another person just based on their looks. Socks with sandals: you're a dad. Constant cargo shorts: you smoke a lot of weed. Red hair: you're loosely related to Satan and are part of the undead army. Look, we all have our "thing," and, as a redhead, our thing just happens to come with the assumption that we are a little bit dangerous. So how did the mere color of our hair result in the idea that not all is right in Gingerville?

DEFINITION: More recently thought of as a redhead who lacks a soul.

NOTED SATANIC REDS IN POP CULTURE: Syndrome in *The Incredibles*, the Red Queen in Tim Burton's *Alice in Wonderland*, and Hilly Holbrook in *The Help*, to name a few.

HOW IT HAPPENED:

Biblical art tells us a lot about how redheads have historically been perceived. For women, Eve (ya know, of Adam and Eve) was often depicted with long red hair by artists like Raphael in *The Temptation of Adam and Eve*. As a reminder, she committed the first sin and condemned us all to a life outside paradise. So, yeah, she can definitely breed some resentment and be seen as an evil biblical figure. While for men, the real kiss of death came in the form of Judas Iscariot. The dude who essentially sentenced Jesus to death is unequivocally considered evil. And so, of course, we see Judas more often than not shown with red hair, as in Carl Bloch's *The Last Supper*, or in Giacomo Raffaelli's mosaic copy of Leonardo da Vinci's *Last Supper*. And, more recently, Harvey Keitel played the role of Judas in *The Last Temptation of Christ*, and I bet you already know the magic hair color Judas had in that film . . . ding ding ding! Red for the win! Now as to *why* Judas keeps getting

Being a ginger has plagued me my entire life. People say I smell like copper. I can get a sunburn indoors at night. According to recent legend, I have no soul.

EMMA,
GLEE

Carl Heinrich Bloch, via Wikimedia Commons, *The Last Supper*

the ginger treatment, there's no one specific answer. But lingering stereotypes likely have something to do with it. Those biblical renderings likely influenced our malicious depiction in pop culture, like the character of Fagin in *Oliver Twist*, who's total and pure evil, or all those redheaded vampires in Anne Rice's *Vampire Chronicles*. Some myths just can't seem to die . . . (See what I did there?) The truth is that people have long feared what they don't understand. And for many people, the very idea of red hair is hard to comprehend. It's so bright! And red! How could it be anything other than the result of witchcraft?! It's not our fault that norms couldn't handle our gorgeous locks, and luckily we now have science to prove that red hair isn't the result of the devil, but simple genetics.

OUR POP CULTURE PERSONA:

When you're trying to remember evil reds in pop culture, you don't have to throw the memory stick too far. After all, there's no denying the flaming red hair of the Chucky doll in those *Child's Play* films, or similarly the bright red locks on Junior in *Problem Child*. In the '90s I grew up with Roger from *Doug* and an entire bullying family, the O'Doyles, in *Billy Madison*. And this trope is gender neutral, as it applies to men and women. Just remember Poison Ivy from the Batman series or Big Red in *Bring It On*. It's a very real and present stereotype.

Whether it's animated evil, like Prince Hans in *Frozen*, or live action (looking at you, Victoria from those *Twilight* movies), we're seemingly all evil, all the time. Which can be a problem when you start to associate red hair with malevolence. Because when people watch Michael C. Hall on *Dexter* and notice his ginger-kissed locks as he's brutally killing people, they might see a redhead out in the wild and pause (just for the briefest of moments) to wonder if we're all alike.

> You know I read online that Judas was a redhead. I don't trust any one of them. Every time I see Reba McEntire I just want to shout, "You killed my Lord and savior."
>
> THE NEW NORMAL

> It's hard for redheads to make friends, because people subconsciously think they're evil.
>
> CRAWFORD WHITTEMORE, DADS

WHAT IT MEANS FOR REDHEADS

Of course, the thing to remember here is **#notallredheads**. We aren't naturally evil or bullies in real life. In fact, if Kick a Ginger Day is any indication—and, yes, that's a real holiday we'll get into more later—it's the redheads who are being bullied rather than the other way around. But that doesn't mean that people won't assume we're evil or say hurtful things to our faces. (If I had a dollar for every time someone suggested I didn't have a soul, I'd be writing this from my space mansion on Mars.)

There's no real way to get rid of this trope just yet, but it's up to each individual redhead to decide what they're going to do with it. And if anyone out there wants to start a redhead uprising, count me in.

HOW TO RESPOND TO IT

When someone accuses you of being a soulless vampire, don't hesitate to use one of these:

1. "That's right, I don't have a soul. It'll be nice to outlive you."
2. "Yeah, it's cool if you call me evil, so long as you don't mind me bringing you to hell."
3. "I actually have the Devil on speed dial, should I give him a call and relay what you just said to me?"

5. The Animated Ginger

Let's pour some tea and spill about animation's obsession with red hair. Go ahead, think of all the Disney and Pixar films you've seen. Now think of all the redheads in those films. Or, in the case of *Brave*, a whole clan of gingers. To put things in perspective, redhead Disney princesses currently outnumber brunette ones. Princesses with black hair are in the lead, followed by blondes, then redheads, then brunettes. Again, with just 2 percent of the world's population being ginger, what made us worthy of having four princesses—Merida, Anna, Megara, and Ariel—to call our own?

DEFINITION: A redhead, but in the form of a delightfully nimble animated character.

KEY ANIMATED GINGERS IN POP CULTURE: Merida, Peter Pan, Hercules, Kim Possible, Princess Fiona, and so many more—seriously, there are too many to list.

For one, the color red is eye-catching, and when you're making an animated movie, you want each character to distinctly stand out. Enter red hair, which, as we all know, is an easy way to differentiate someone from the rest of the herd. We are noticeable, whether it be in real life or when we're drawn that way. And that's likely a huge deciding factor as to why we're inserted into so many animated films. If you want a lead who really makes an entrance, you give Linguini from *Ratatouille* red hair. Or if you want to show that a character is a bit of a spitfire—fiery tempers, right?—an animator might throw in some red, like Jessie from *Toy Story* or Ellie from *Up*. Depicting animated characters as redheads is a creative decision that signals importance to the audience, and it's definitely not an accident.

HOW IT HAPPENED:

It may seem like the real Disney redhead revolution began with *The Little Mermaid* in 1989, but it began long before Ariel was ever dreamed into existence. It all started in 1940 with the character of Lampwick in *Pinocchio*—he was one of Pinocchio's friends and impossible to miss with that bright red hair. Up next was *Fantasia*, and there were two redhead characters: the Vulcan and one of the Satyrs. In 1941's *The Reluctant Dragon* both the Boy and the Father were gingers, and that same year the character of Smitty in *Dumbo* also had, you guessed it, red hair. In 1950, *Cinderella* arrived and her evil stepsister, Anastasia, just so happened to be ginger. Then came *Peter Pan* in 1953, which was incredibly valuable to the ginger cause, since it featured Peter (a ginger) and gave us our first leading redhead man in animation. Another redhead came our way with Anita Radcliffe in 1961's *One Hundred and One Dalmatians*, followed by *The Sword in the Stone* in 1963, which featured two redheads in Sir Kay and his father, Sir Ector. In 1973, *Robin Hood* featured a ginger as the title character (albeit, a fox, but Robin Hood was also most definitely a red fox). And in 1977, *The Rescuers* debuted with the evil antagonist Madame Medusa and her intensely bright red hair.

The '80s were another big decade for gingers in Disney animated films; Tod and Vixey from *The Fox and the Hound* in 1981; Taran, Orddu, Orwen, and Orgoch from 1985's *The Black Cauldron*; and Jenny, Oliver, and Fagin in 1988's *Oliver and Company*. Only after all of those ginger predecessors did Ariel from *The Little Mermaid* hit our screens in 1989. Undoubtedly, she's one of our most memorable animated icons, but the obsession was there long before her perfect sea hair appeared.

Princess Merida: "I climbed up the Crown's Tooth and drank from the fire falls."
King Fergus: "Did you, now? They say only the ancient kings were brave enough to drink the fire."

BRAVE

The redhead revolution also occurred at Pixar, and their obsession can be traced back to 1999 with the release of *Toy Story 2* and the introduction of Jessie. Underneath that cowgirl hat was one very red braid, and the rest is now animated history. In 2003, *Finding Nemo* gave us a ginger in the form of Darla Sherman, and the next year brought us Syndrome in *The Incredibles*. Alfredo Linguini in 2007's *Ratatouille* had dark auburn hair. The following year Mary in *Wall-E* graced the screen with a little red ponytail. And then in 2009 we saw Ellie with her tinge of ginge in *Up*. In 2012 came *Brave*, a.k.a. a love song to red hair, with Merida, King Fergus, and Merida's three younger brothers all crowned with magnetic red locks. And in 2015, Meg, the best friend in *Inside Out*, practically had a halo of red curls wrapped around her head. Obsessed much, animation?

OUR POP CULTURE PERSONA:

It's now no secret that animation and red hair go together like marshmallows and chocolate. But just how prevalent is this today? There are over thirty leading or recurring characters with red hair in the Disney and Pixar universe. That's a lot of characters! While it may be rare to see a natural redhead out in the wild, turn on an animated film and you're guaranteed to see us. And for many people around the world, seeing a redhead in an animated movie may be a person's first encounter with the visual image of a redhead. So our presence in animated form truly does have an impact, not just on pop culture, but on other people's perception of us.

WHAT IT MEANS FOR REDHEADS

Little known fact:* the song "Part of Your World" that Ariel sings in the grotto

---

* Maybe.

was actually about redheads just wanting to feel they weren't so alone in the universe. And not feeling alone is exactly what happens when, as a redhead, you see someone who even vaguely resembles you on-screen. Even seeing an animated someone and not a flesh-and-blood someone, makes the difference between feeling isolated and knowing you're not alone. Because as a redhead, we are often the only one in our immediate families with red hair, or the only person at school or work with it, so having representation can make a huge impact.

In fact, it's usually our pop culture icons that drive us in life, especially when we're younger. They're who we dress as for Halloween. Their songs are the ones we sing when we're dancing alone in our room. And they're who we quietly aspire to be, for better or worse. As such, it's important to keep in mind that while the animated characters on-screen may resemble us, they don't need to define us. (Unless your true calling in life is to be a mermaid, in which case, break a fin!)

HOW TO RESPOND TO IT

For those moments when someone asks if your favorite princess is Ariel, here's all you need to say:

1. "I refuse to answer that on the grounds of #notallredheads."
2. "Yes, and if you say she's your favorite too, I think we'll have to be best friends."
3. "I understand that you're jealous because redheads have the best Disney princess, but don't put that on me."

When Your Disney Obsession Goes Too Far

There comes a time in every person's life when they find that special someone. Some may use the term soul mate, while others just know it as that moment when you've found "the one." For me, I found my one true love when I was eight years old, and that person was Ariel from *The Little Mermaid*.

She and I were basically domestic partners. I made time to watch her movie every day, and I'd seen *The Little Mermaid* enough to know that the amount of times I'd watched it was unhealthy. Because there was no actual reason for me to be able to mouth every word and mimic all the individual characters' movements. I was struggling to get above a C in my third-grade math class, but I was acing being a fake part of Ariel's world.

I also thought we had a lot in common: the red hair, our love of forks, and our burning obsession with Prince Eric. He was perfect. With that mop of inky hair, his ocean-blue eyes, and that undone button that revealed a hairless chest—what more could you want? Most important of all: he had a thing for redheads. I'm only slightly ashamed to say that I nicknamed a pillow "Prince Eric" and would queue up that lagoon scene so I could kiss Pillow Prince Eric at the exact moment when Ariel nearly sealed the deal. Socially awkward preteens trying to wade through a sea of confusing hormones—gotta love 'em.

As I moved on to high school I became "older and wiser," so I made the sophisticated move of swapping the daily VHS tape for regular singalongs with *The Little Mermaid* soundtrack in my car. But without my realizing it, my Ariel fixation began to affect other parts of my life. Like, with my first real-life, non-animated crush, Ben. He had the swoop of hair, the million-watt smile, and (even though we had to wear Catholic school uniforms) I could see his chest was hairless through his one undone button. What more could I want? That was all the proof I needed: Prince Eric was real, and he was going to like me.

So I did what any rational fourteen-year-old girl would: I stalked the shit out of him. He was on the student council, so I joined too. I discovered that he was a math tutor, so suddenly I needed help with my homework. His number was listed in our school directory, so I called and breathed heavily into the phone whenever he picked up. Ya know, normal stuff. But no matter what I did, Ben barely noticed. I mean, he was my Prince Eric, wasn't this supposed to work out in the end?

Then I posed a very important question to myself: WWAD? (What Would Ariel Do?) And I knew the answer: she'd use her voice. Luckily there were no sea witches trying to steal mine at the time, so I decided to do just that. It was after school, and I saw Ben about to get into his red Ford Mustang. I'd just popped a mint and was feeling really confident about the black choker I'd picked to wear that morning. As I walked up, the rest happened in slow motion, the same way seeing him for the first time played out. He smiled, I smiled, and then I leaned slightly against his car and said, "Hey, kinda random, but would you wanna go out sometime?" His smile remained as he politely leaned in and whispered, "That's really sweet, but no."

Yeah, I got rejected by my Disney prince. And the most annoying part was that it was my own damn fault. I was so blinded by his beauty that I didn't want to accept what was as clear as the word "no" coming out of his mouth: we had nothing in common. He didn't like me and had never shown any interest in me. And I knew nothing about him other than the fact that he was my IRL Prince Eric. But I'd become so delusional about what he could be, based on his animated persona, that I wasn't able to comprehend that he was a human and not a Disney prince.

Which is to say that I learned my lesson: pick your icons wisely. And, really, there are plenty of redheads to idolize in the sea (and no judgments if you still go for the mermaid one)!

6. *The Lead Ginge*

A famous redhead once sang, "The sun will come out tomorrow," and, indeed, our time to shine has arrived. Because, regardless of some of the stereotypes we've faced, the real silver lining is that redheads are taking on much larger roles than ever before. The world is really beginning to appreciate us in the way we're meant to be worshipped, and we need to start owning our newfound power.

DEFINITION: The star! The real tour de force! The redhead who, in essence, everyone wants to be.

KEY REDHEAD STARS IN POP CULTURE: Our queen, Julianne Moore; our princess, Jessica Chastain; our king, Robert Redford; and our prince, Domhnall Gleeson.

Sure, the stereotypes we've gone over still exist, but the point is there's a new and even better "stereotype" emerging. That would be the trope of having a redhead as the lead. Meaning we don't need to embody just one type or characteristic. We gingers can be flawed, compelling, and, well, *normal* human beings. And now that the walls have been broken down around having a redhead as the lead, it'll only continue to get better from here.

HOW IT HAPPENED:

It's hard to pinpoint exactly when this pop culture shift started. For the ladies, having actors like Amy Adams and Emma Stone were a magnificent help. Sure, they may not be naturally red, but they adopted our look, and when they continued to land leading roles, they mostly stuck to that color. Which unintentionally told audiences that our red hair was something they should get used to and even fond of.

> This class is like a redhead that drinks scotch and loves Die Hard. *I suggest you all get her number.*
>
> COMMUNITY

For the men, the leading roles have been slightly more recent. We'll start with Domhnall Gleeson—he's a classic and utterly gorgeous redhead man, and he played a leading romantic love interest in *About Time* (2013). That was groundbreaking because he was the first redhead man to play a romantic lead in a rom-com. Before him there was romantic lead Robert Redford, but he was never in a rom-com. Domnhall was the first, and now he won't be the last because he proved that ginger men are not only sweet, funny, and charming on-screen, but that they can be sexy as hell while doing so. My fellow redheads already knew this fact, but now the world is realizing it too. That we even have a leading redhead man to worship is kind of a miracle in itself, and proof that change is happening all around us. That's because ginger men are so often relegated to the sidekick role, it's rare to see them as anything else. But it's not just Domhnall who's getting top billing now—btw, he also starred in *Ex Machina* (2015) and *Star Wars: Episode VII* (2015) —Adonis Damian Lewis also changed the game when he played Nicholas Brody in *Homeland*, and Bobby Axelrod on *Billions*. We've definitely had our share of trailblazers in the past few years, and that trend is only going to keep moving upward.

> *This is an historic moment. And I'm not talking about this first-female-President thing. I'm talking about the first redhead press secretary!*
>
> VEEP

OUR POP CULTURE PERSONA:

The redhead landscape has changed. Like, if you look at Kimmy in *Unbreakable Kimmy Schmidt*, we see the classic comedic redhead. But you know what else she is? Asexual and completely innocent, which isn't something that's always assumed about redheads (as we know!). And instead of fiery redheads, we're seeing women who are just plain strong as hell. Like Jessica Chastain's role as Maya in *Zero Dark Thirty*, where she plays a CIA operative who's hell-bent on finding Osama bin Laden. She could potentially fall under that fiery redhead category, but she's so thoughtful and brilliant in her strategy that she instead veers into that badass territory. The same goes for Claire in *Jurassic World*, played by Bryce Dallas Howard. She's a boss, wears heels, AND fights off dinosaurs—it doesn't get more bang-up than that. And then there's Giselle in *Enchanted*, played by Amy Adams—she was just a straight-up leading lady. No stereotypes about her. Or Mireille Enos's Alice on *The Catch*, who's a private investigator with little tolerance for bullshit. So, yeah, loads of examples here.

HOW TO RESPOND TO IT

When someone correctly recognizes that we're awesome as fuck, here's what to do:

1. "I bet you say that to all the redheads."
2. "Between you and me, the genie granted my wish."
3. "Marry me?"

WHAT IT MEANS FOR REDHEADS

Like that one fruit fly you just can't seem to get rid of, those old stereotypes about redheads will continue to linger, no matter how hard you swat at them. But we can see that the more redheads appear on TV and on film, the more things change and evolve to fit the truth—that we're everyday people. And seeing representations of that in pop culture will eventually help dispel a lot of the long-held beliefs people have about us.

She's a redhead.
I love redheads.

BEN,
THE SECRET LIFE OF THE
AMERICAN TEENAGER

two

All the Red Science You Ever Wanted

We're Secret Superheroes

R edheads, of course, are human. We are living, breathing humans, just like everyone else. But what I'm suggesting is…maybe we have something special that the rest of humanity doesn't? In the same way that celebrities, kittens, and cookie cakes have that certain sparkly glow about them—OK, we don't exactly have *that* glow, but we're definitely close to it. The point being that there are real, scientific facts to back up everything you've suspected about redheads being physically extraordinary. And those facts prove that we have strengths that make us IRL superheroes. For so long we've known that there was something unusual about our bodies, and now we're going to get into the nitty-gritty of it.

REDHEADS ARE *TECHNICALLY* MUTANTS

HUMANS   RED-
          HEADS   SUPER-
                   HUMANS

Being part of the X-Men isn't for everyone, and it's certainly not a choice. For redheads in particular, the mutant life chose you. That's right, gingers are actually, physically, and genetically different, thanks to one very important gene called *MC1R*. Remember that gene, *MC1R*, because we're going to be talking about it. A. LOT. Let's get a little into the specifics of what this means, because you're a smart person, and smart people like to learn things. Our genes are sometimes called the blueprint for life, because they make proteins that tell our bodies how to act and develop. In short, they're very important. And in norms, the *MC1R* gene produces a protein called melanin that determines the pigmentation of hair and skin.

But in the late '90s, scientists discovered that redheads have a mutation on the *MC1R* gene. Because of that mutation, *MC1R* doesn't produce melanin in redheads but, instead, produces a protein called pheomelanin. That protein is directly responsible for our hair color and can often influence other things like fair skin and freckles. Though red hair isn't limited to Caucasian people— there are gingers of color naturally occurring in places like Morocco, Papua New Guinea, and elsewhere.

Regardless of race, the *MC1R* gene probably also accounts for our superhuman strength and ability to shoot beams from our eyes.[*]

WE DON'T NEED *AS MUCH* SUN TO MAKE VITAMIN D

You may have heard a rumor that redheads are vampires because you rarely see us out in the sun. And while I'm not prepared to deny those allegations (hey, if we can live forever, I'm not going to question it), it's also important to point out that we frankly don't need to be in the sun as much.

REDHEAD SECRET:
We don't need to be outside for as long as norms.

Thanks to evolution, and a higher concentration of red hair and pale skin in some cloudy European environments, redheads developed a stronger ability to create their own vitamin D in their bodies. (Survival of the fittest, and everything.) So, when redheads do go outside, they're able to produce more vitamin D in a shorter amount of time than those with other hair colors. While a ginger may need just ten to fifteen minutes outside, a brunette may need significantly more time to make the same amount of vitamin D.

This gives us an evolutionary advantage, since low levels of vitamin D can lead to things like rickets, diabetes, and arthritis. Which means we may live even longer, so therefore it's only right to conclude that we may be vamp . . . really fun in old age.

---

[*] Not scientifically proven . . . yet.

REDHEADS *SMELL* DIFFERENT
(AND ARGUABLY BETTER)

Sniff, sniff, sniff. What's that? The delightful smell of reds being the roses of the human world? Why, yes, we do smell better than norms, and let me explain why. The first recorded evidence of this was from Dr. Augustin Galopin in his 1886 book, *Le parfum de la femme*. The book and his findings were based on experimentation and observations, which means they aren't entirely scientific. But one of his theories was that every woman gave off a specific bouquet of scents based solely on hair color. When he tested this theory out on redheads, he was able to detect that we have our own particular scent. For reds or women with chestnut hair, Galopin observed their scent to be that of ambergris, an earthy and sensual scent.[4]

> While the rest of the species is descended from apes, redheads are descended from cats.
>
> MARK TWAIN

Designed by Freepik

And Dr. Galopin, as it turns out, wasn't entirely wrong. Because scent is different when you have red hair, especially when you apply a scent to your skin. While perfume on a blonde or brunette will smell the same, any scent you put on a red's skin will smell different. To be clear: this bizarre phenomenon is only true of redheads, and it's the result of our unique biochemistry. To explain this a bit, let's start with this fact: everyone has a skin mantle. A skin mantle is secreted by our sebaceous glands and acts as a thin acidic film on the surface of our skin to protect us from bacteria and other contaminants. So, in other words, if you take a look at any body part covered in skin you'll have this thin acidic film that the eye can't see. But, for whatever reason, a red's skin mantle is more acidic than those of any other hair color. Not only does this increased acidity cause whatever we put on our skin to smell different, but scents also don't last as long on us reds.[5] So while we may not smell the same as everyone else, if what Dr. Galopin noted is true, then we've got the sensual scent of ambergris on our side.

> **PRO TIP:** If you want a scent to have some longevity as a red, spritz a bit in your hair.

REDHEAD WOMEN HANDLE PAINKILLERS
BETTER THAN EVERYONE ELSE

If Beyoncé has taught us anything, it's that women run the world, so it shouldn't be all that surprising to hear that we're the tougher of the sexes. This is especially true for redhead ladies, who have a leg up on the whole handling-pain thing.

A 2003 study tested how women of various hair colors handled painkillers, the theory being that while all women experience pain in the same way, redheaded women have an added benefit when pain-killing drugs are introduced. So, let's say you have a headache. When your body feels that pain, the brain automatically releases natural opiates (very similar to morphine) to try and make your life better. But there's still pain, so you take a pill for that pain. In most people, when this happens, those natural opiates interfere with whatever drugs you take to calm the pain, and in that way make the drugs less effective.

WHO'S STRONGER?

While we believe pain is the same in all women of all hair colors, our study shows women with red hair respond better to the pain-killing drug we tested than anyone else—including men.

MCGILL UNIVERSITY STUDY

However, what the McGill University study found was that when redheaded women release natural opiates, we're able to do so without their interfering with the drugs we take. Meaning that we have the added boost of all those natural opiates, plus the drugs' full potential. When taking pain-killing drugs, redheaded women can tolerate up to 25 percent more pain than people with other hair colors as a result of this, which (to take a smidge of artistic license here) means that when you ask, "Who run the world?" it's redhead girls.

REDHEAD WOMEN FEEL *LESS* STINGING PAIN (LIKE NEEDLES)

What can I say, boys, life isn't fair. Except if you're a redhead lady, because then life is extremely fair. It was a 2011 study out of Oslo University that found redheaded women feel less pain when pricked by a pin than those with other hair colors do. (Only women were tested in this study, so there's a chance that this could apply to ginger men too! Time and more studies will tell.) So, what does that mean? Basically when it comes to stinging pain, like a needle in the arm, or anything where the pain is at the surface of the skin, we're better able to handle it.

REDHEAD SECRET:
Ginger women don't feel the pain of a needle as much as norms.

Scientists aren't totally sure why this happens. It's one of those unexplained mysteries, like Area 51 and the Loch Ness monster. But they think it might have something to do with the mutation on that *MC1R* gene. All we know is that when it comes to pain, ginger ladies are killing the game.

YOU MAY *SECRETLY* BE A REDHEAD

If you're reading this, then chances are you're either a redhead or aspire to be one someday. But with redheads making up a select 2 percent of the world's population, not everyone is so lucky. Though there is some promising news for norms: it turns out that plenty of norms actually carry the ginger gene. That's right: you might be a covert ginger! Red hair is recessive, which means that while you may not personally have red hair, you may be a carrier of the mutated *MC1R* gene. So basically this gives you covert reds the capacity to do great things. And by great things, I mean produce more redheads.

4 IN 10 PEOPLE CARRY THE REDHEAD GENE

To give you an idea of just how many walk among us tagged with this lucky gene, it's estimated that four in ten people carry it. And a project conducted by Britain's DNA, a genetic testing company, found that in the United Kingdom alone there are 20 million ginger-gene carriers—although only 4 percent of the UK population actually has red hair. So, what I'm saying is: there's no time like the present to see if your offspring will win the genetic lotto. Go find yourself a redhead to settle down with. It'll certainly give you an advantage when you attend our annual redhead summit dinners! By invite only, of course.

REDHEADS KNOW WHEN IT'S GETTING COLD WELL BEFORE YOU DO

We're also the groundhogs of humans, because we'll tell you right away if it's going to stay cold or if things are looking warmer. The deal is that when it comes to temperature, redheads feel the extremes of both cold and superwarm temperatures more than anyone else. It was a 2005 study from the University of Louisville that led researchers to discover this hidden gift. And they hypothesize that the ginger gene (good old *MC1R*) may be causing the temperature-detecting gene to become overactivated, making redheads more sensitive to the cold and heat. So if a redhead tells you they're feeling a bit chilly, you better grab a blanket and hold on tight, because *winter is coming*.

WE DON'T GO GRAY AS FAST AS OTHER COLORS

There's a long-held rumor in the redhead community that gingers don't go gray and that our hair instead turns white. And the thing about being a magical unicorn is that you don't exactly want to give up all of your mysteries, but in the spirit of honesty, I'll tell you: we do gray, just like any other hair color. In fact, I just recently found my first gray, which I've come to name Pearl. But because of our lack of melanin, the hair can appear almost blonde, and then turn gray. So what we're dealing with here is really a sleight of hand when it comes to hair color. In a way, our grays blend in better with our hair than gray hair in a person with dark hair. It's just one of the added benefits we have at our disposal.

RED IS THE HARDEST COLOR TO FAKE

We're the easiest hair color to spot in a crowd, but we're also the hardest color to get from a bottle. The struggle for fake redheads is *real*. If you've ever dyed your hair, then it's no shocker to hear that the color will fade, as all colors do. But red hair dye tends to fade faster than the rest. Why is that? Well, red is a more intense hue, and the bolder the color, the faster it fades. Also, as celebrity hair stylist Danny Moon told *InStyle*,[6] the dye molecules found in red hair dye are larger than those in other hues. Which means when you try to dye someone's hair red, those larger molecules can't penetrate the hair as deeply as the smaller molecules in other colors can. And that hair hardship should make natural redheads appreciate their own bold hue all the more, right?

WE'RE *HARDER* TO SEDATE DURING SURGERY

Some people go down easy—give them a NyQuil and you won't see them again for a week. But redheads? We're rebellious. Research is still being done on this, but a 2004 University of Louisville study found that it takes 20 percent more general anesthesia during surgery, on average, to sedate a redhead. Which, on the one hand, can be a bit stressful for a redhead to think about—I don't know about you, but I'd like to be sedated during any surgery—and on the other, is a pretty cool and weird fluke of our bodies. So far, there's no sure answer as to why this happens to us—it may be that *MC1R* at work again—but you've gotta give us a lot more if you want the lights out.

REDHEADS NEED 20% MORE GENERAL ANESTHESIA DURING SURGERY

AND WE NEED *MORE* NOVOCAIN AT THE DENTIST

Nothing against dentists—if not for them, we'd all be eating applesauce through a straw—but they're just scary as hell. The instruments, the bright light, that bubble-gum-flavored topical gel . . . no one really likes it. Here's the thing, though, redheads actually have an excuse beyond the bubble-gum taste.

In 2005, another University of Louisville study found that, much like with anesthesia, we require more topical numbing at the dentist. So while a brunette may only need one shot of Novocain to go numb, we may need two, or three, or so much that our entire face is numb. Which I can tell you from personal experience, makes eating a harrowing endeavor. Scientists aren't sure why this is happening, but one thing is clear: we're not just going to roll over and let some dentist (sorry, dentists) drill into our mouths.

LIST OF CURRENT REDHEAD SUPERPOWERS

☆ Because of our mutated *MC1R* gene, reds are actually mutants, not unlike the X-Men.

☆ We can make vitamin D in our bodies at a much faster rate than the norms.

☆ We know when winter is coming, because we sense cold and heat better than everyone else.

☆ On average, we smell different (and arguably better) than the norms.

☆ We have the gift of looking like we're going gray at a much slower rate.

☆ And if you try to dye your hair red, you'll have a helluva time keeping that shade.

☆ We require 20 percent more anesthesia during surgery.

☆ And we also need more anesthesia at the dentist.

☆ Pain-killing drugs work better on red women than everyone else.

☆ And red women feel the sting of a needle less than blond or dark-haired women.

☆ There are norms who walk among us and secretly carry the redhead gene.

☆ And we can leap tall buildings in a single bound . . . though that's yet to be scientifically proved.

How to Get Out of a Dental Visit, Kinda

A trip to the dentist for anyone is a lot like being called to the principal's office—you know you've probably done something wrong, and the visit involves a whole lot of bargaining with higher powers. But if we're being honest: I hated the dentist. "Hate" is a strong word. It invokes images of plotting revenge in a winding high tower or being filled with the kind of venom that could melt people into puddles. And yet "hate" is still the word that accurately describes how I felt about the dentist.

The problem was that I was in a deeply committed relationship with sugar. I loved Pixy Stix, Laffy Taffy, Skittles, Blow Pops, and in particular the bite-size caramels you could buy at the drugstore from the nickel bin. And while I was head over heels in love with sugar, we were in a bit of an abusive relationship. I ate sugar every day. I gave it my time, my energy, and all of my devotion. But what did sugar offer me in return? Cavities, and big bunches of them. By the time I was thirteen, I'd already had seven filled. And I knew the drill, so to speak: sit on the plastic-covered seat, close your eyes, listen to the sounds of Celine Dion crooning over the radio, and get three to four shots of Novocain in your mouth. I knew this was unusually high because every time the dentist picked up the sharp needle that would "help the pain," he lamented that he never had to give this much to any of his other patients. I got the impression that he thought I was making it up when I'd kick my legs and gargle through his fingers, "I can still feel it!" But I could, in fact, still feel the drill.

So I'd understandably started to sweat this one time when I was on my way to the dentist to get yet another cavity filled. My mom was driving because, ya know, pesky minimum-age laws. But that gave me ample time to scheme my way out of the nightmare situation that is, for redheads, so many shots of Novocain. I'd like to say that I handled attending the dentist appointment with grace—the kind of cool, calm, and collected typically reserved for royalty on their wedding day—but I was thirteen, and also a redhead who had a reason to be filled with dread. Which is why, as my mom stepped out of the car, I took the opportunity to lock her out of it, keeping myself (and the keys) inside. I know: I locked my mom out of a car. I'm a terrible person. Whatever. But as I'd vehemently explained to her on the drive over, I didn't want to do this. There had to be another way—maybe we could tie some string around my teeth and just yank them all out—dentures wouldn't be *so* bad.

In hindsight, this was not a wise decision. For one, it stressed my poor, patient mother out. And I'm not totally sure what I thought this would accomplish. I mean, I couldn't live in the car forever . . . could I? Eventually, the dentist, his assistant, and my mother all surrounded me. I sat, cross-armed and steadfast in the front seat while the dentist politely explained that they'd just gotten something called "laughing gas," (a.k.a. nitrous oxide), which would likely make the whole experience of getting a cavity filled much easier.

Admittedly, the dentist was right—the laughing gas did help during the appointment. While I still needed the same amount of Novocain, the addition of the new sedative effectively erased the rest of the experience. Instead of fixating on the sound of the drill, I was high out of my mind and essentially not in the dentist's chair.

Moral of the story? Laughing gas is pretty great.

three

Red-Hot Sex Talk

How People Think You'll Be in Bed vs. How You Actually Are

F un fact: redheads have sex. I know it can be a little shocking to realize that unicorns have time for such wanton pursuits, but that's why I'm here: to set the record straight. Now some of you reading this may love to talk about sex. If you're one of these people, please be my friend, as we'll have a lot in common. But if you're one of those clutching your pearls at the mere thought of some sensible sex talk, you may want to find your fainting couch now, because it's time to chat about sexy sex things.

And more specifically, how being a redhead gives you a leg up, so to speak, when it comes to getting down to business. Now you may be thinking that this sounds like a load of fake beans, because how can something like hair color affect anything sexual? But it's true. For example, remember from the last chapter that reds feel temperature changes more keenly than anyone else. And because we've all got a dirty mind somewhere, it's not hard to imagine what that temperature sensitivity could translate to in the bedroom.

> *You can sleep with a blonde, you can sleep with a brunette, but you'll never get any sleep with a redhead.*
>
> JAMIE LUNER,
> ACTRESS

As a redhead, our sexuality can be a little uncomfortable to think about, especially since so many norms take an active role in discussing it. Like, how many other people have to deal with the color of their pubes (i.e., "firecrotch") being a topic of conversation? But the point is that if we actually talk about these things and debunk some of the myths surrounding us, it'll take away the taboo nature of it all. We can discuss it here, in this safe space, with the assurance that there are no judgments and the knowledge that every red approaches sex differently. There's just a lot of rumors about redheads when it comes to sex, and it's time to put those to bed.

NEVER HAVE I EVER: *Ginger Edition*

THE RULES

- Grab a drink.
- If you've done the thing, take a sip.
- If you haven't, sit back and judge.

Ever played this game? You know the one. You're with your friends, having some beverages, and one clever little monkey of a person suggests playing Never Have I Ever. It's the game where someone says something they've never done, and if you've done that thing, you take a drink. If you haven't, you simply sit back and get to judge everyone who's sipping from their cups. It's fun and silly, and since sex is often just along those lines, we're going to play a game of Never Have I Ever: Ginger Edition. Feel free to also use this as an excuse to pour yourself a glass of something nice—and remember the rules: take a big sip if any of these ring true to you.

 NEVER HAVE I EVER been called crazy in bed.

Anyone other than me take a drink? This is probably one of the more dominant rumors about redheads: as soon as we get you alone, we're going to lead you into our sex dungeon and show you things you've never seen. It's not unusual for someone to casually suggest that we're wild in the sack or assume that we're going to be. And it ties back in large part to that whole stereotype of redheads as vixens. You can't watch a TV series or binge some films for long before stumbling into this stereotype.

I remember acknowledging it for the first time when I watched *American Pie* and saw a red-haired character named Michelle (played by Alyson Hannigan). Even if you haven't seen the film, you've probably heard all about how this one time, at band camp, Michelle stuck a flute up her . . . well, we all can imagine where she stuck that flute. It was an iconic film moment, and that line really stuck with people, to say the least. Things with Michelle and her sexuality escalated quickly when the lead character, Jim (played by Jason Biggs), asked her to prom. In one particularly memorable scene, we see Michelle and Jim in bed, about to seal the deal on prom night. Michelle's foot kicks over a lamp as she climbs on top of Jim and yells, "What's my name? Say my name, bitch!" And Jim, helpless to her ways, can do little more than yell back, "Michelle! Michelle!"

It's a funny scene. They set up Michelle as a bit of a dud throughout the movie, and then, all of a sudden, you get her into a bedroom and WHAM, she's a total sexpot. I laughed, as did a lot of other people in the theater. What I didn't anticipate was that for years after that film came out, I'd continue to get comparisons to Michelle. "I bet you're like that girl in *American Pie*, huh?" I was once asked at a bar, years later.

It's fair to argue that these assumptions about us might actually lead to our being more open with sex. If people expect you to be a little kinkier in the bedroom and pursue you for that very reason, you might be game to try those things out. Yeah, maybe you never really thought of yourself as the S&M type, but since your partner brought it up . . . sure, why not give it a go. And if people feel more comfortable bringing up what they'd like to do in bed with you, because they think you're wilder than the rest, then it's more likely to yield actual results.

So who knows: maybe we are better in bed than everyone else. Maybe, on average, we're a little more down to try things out. But some of us are just fine with ordering off the regular-sex menu. Regardless, norms will probably still think of us as being adventurous types—it's just up to us reds to decide if we actually are.

 NEVER HAVE I EVER had someone suggest I'm promiscuous.

Depending on the kinds of ginger circles you run in, you may have had someone tell you that redheads have more sex. Or that we're slutty and more likely to hop into bed quicker than other people. If you're a red, maybe this has manifested itself when you're out at a bar, and you can't help but notice that everyone who hits on you looks shocked if you say thanks but no thanks to going home with them. The stereotype that redheads have more fun has also been confirmed by studies—but the important question is this: have these studies been influenced by the stereotypes too? Let's explore!

There are two recent studies that confirm the idea that redheads are more promiscuous than those with any other hair color. And when you hear things like "a study confirmed" and "there were two of them," it starts to seem a little like, wow, this stereotype must be true, right? But when you take a closer look, not all is right in finger-pointing Studyville. We'll start with the 2006 study out of Germany, which claimed it interviewed hundreds of women and found that red-haired ladies had more partners and were more sexually active than women with other hair colors. But let's get some things straight about this:

✦ The study wasn't published in any reputable science journal, which suggests the science behind it isn't entirely sound. (If real scientists won't go near it with an eyeglass, then something smells off.)

✦ It's not clear from the study where Dr. Werner Habermehl (the doctor who conducted this) actually works, and there's no indication as to where the study took place. So whether or not it involved any university, think tank, or research institute (which is typical of most studies) remains unclear.

- Whether or not the redheads interviewed for this had dyed red hair or were natural redheads is never discussed. So half, or all, of the respondents could be dye jobs, which obviously doesn't reflect on natural gingers.

- There are also no statistics surrounding the study. So how big of a percentage difference between the reds who answered versus the norms is unclear. It could be 70 percent, but it could also be 1 percent. We'll just never know!

- Also, I tried to find Dr. Werner Habermehl. I couldn't. He's like a damn missing person except for this report. So, there's that!

But hark, we have *another* study to address: a more recent one in 2013's Match.com annual Singles in America study. The study surveyed 5,300 unmarried men and women across the country. It found that redheaded women orgasm more than any other hair color (41 percent of the redhead respondents said they achieved orgasm 90–100 percent of the time, compared to 36 percent of blondes, 34 percent of brunettes, and 29 percent of women with black hair). The study also found that redheads think about sex more, have had more threesomes, and also have experienced more one-night stands and friends-with-benefits relationships than those with other hair colors. And as a result of this study, numerous sites, like Yahoo,[7] *Women's Health,*[8] BuzzFeed,[9] PopSugar,[10] and *Shape,*[11] to name a few, reported that redheads have "more fun" than any other hair color. And by "more fun," I mean more sex. Because what these numbers *seem* to suggest is that we are all about that D, or V, or all of the above. But let's look at the facts behind these results, which were graciously provided by Match.com.

MATCH.COM FINDINGS

41% of red haired women achieve orgasm 90-100% of the time.

Women with red hair think about sex more.

Red-haired ladies have had more threesomes.

Ginger women have more one-night stands and friends-with-benefits relationships.

✦ Of the 5,300 people who responded to the study, only 186 identified as female redheads, which makes up just 3.5 percent of the total. So not a huge sample pool.

✦ To add to the small number of respondents, the exact phrasing of the question asked to determine hair color was this: "Currently, what color is your hair?" Meaning that we have no idea if the 186 people who responded were natural or fake redheads.

In both of the studies, it's unclear if the participants are natural redheads, and the surveys only studied women. Which means a more accurate study would need to include our sexy ginger men. Also, as Molly Mulshine noted in her article on this topic in the *Observer*, confirmation bias likely influenced much of these results. Because if you're being told by society that you're more promiscuous and sexual than everyone else, you might more confidently answer questions about sex. And norms who dye their hair red may lean into that redheaded-vixen stereotype more than many natural reds do. Hell, it's even possible the stereotype is the reason why certain people choose to dye their hair red. If anything, having red hair and knowing you're perceived as being more sexual may lead you to have fewer sexual inhibitions and make you more comfortable in the bedroom (which could account for those "reds have more orgasms" numbers). But there's just no proof we actually have more sex than those with other hair colors. If you're a red who still wants to believe in those studies, then, as Dr. Helen Fisher, who served as an advisor on the Match.com study, told me, "Red hair is novel, and men and women are turned on by people who are novel and different."

 NEVER HAVE I EVER BEEN told that redheads are going extinct and need to start procreating.

Are you getting tipsy from all those drinks? I am. Hella tipsy. And I've gotta take a big sip here because there have been plenty of "studies" over the last decade that suggest that within the next hundred years we may no longer exist. Headlines like "'Hot' Redheads Bound for Extinction,"[12] "Requiem for the Redhead: The Next Great Extinction—Carrot Tops,"[13] and "Will Rare Redheads Be Extinct by 2100?"[14] pop up regularly. All suggesting that within a century there won't be any ginger babies—as in we are the last in our line, the sole survivors of the redhead apocalypse—and our hair will be preserved in museums as a color that once existed. (What a sad thought!) As a result of these studies, T-shirts like, "Kiss me, I'm endangered!" started cropping up,

REDHEAD SECRET:
We may not actually have more sex than anyone else.

along with suggestions that, in order to keep the hair color alive, people should actively seek out and date redheads to propagate the species. In other words: have sex with us, because you're our only hope for survival.

But redheads are not going extinct. And whenever these "studies"—most recently conducted by the Oxford Hair Foundation in 2005—come out, there are loads of articles to debunk them. (I use quotes around the word "studies" because they're typically not scientific studies, but PR stunts.) We aren't going extinct because genetics doesn't work the way these studies suggest. Red hair is a recessive gene, but that doesn't mean it's going to become diluted to the point where it won't exist anymore. In fact, it's nearly impossible to breed out of a population, meaning that we'll likely be sticking around.

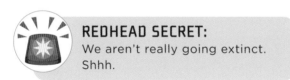

REDHEAD SECRET:
We aren't really going extinct. Shhh.

Not only will reds be sticking around because of genetics, but there's also another theory that might help explain why you'll keep seeing us. If you went through any kind of biology class, then you're likely familiar with Charles Darwin's theory of natural selection, which is basically that certain traits are developed for survival, and the person or animal with the best survival traits will continue to thrive. But Darwin also proposed his sexual selection theory in the same book, *On the Origin of Species*, in 1859. The sexual selection theory is all about the traits humans and animals have that don't help their survival, but do stand out in a crowd, essentially making them more likely to get laid. In other words, there's no survival advantage to a male peacock with bright cerulean blue plumes—those aren't going to help him blend in if there's a predator around. But those plumes are beautiful, and the more different they are from his other male competitors, the more likely it is that he'll be chosen as the female peacock's mate.

THINGS GOING EXTINCT

REDHEADS

Cable TV

Lumbersexuals

The patriarchy

Paleo anything

Raw food diet

Fedoras

Couples meeting IRL

So if we apply sexual selection to humans, the unique traits are what stand out in a sea of beautiful faces. Which is why it's been theorized[15] that the reason redheads have continued to exist is partly due to the fact that we stand out more than any other hue. Norms see us and, like cats drawn to a red laser, can't help being attracted. On top of that, because of our reputation for being rowdy in bed, norms assume that we'll be great mates. The redder the hair, the more fiery we are down there, and what not. So either way: other people's desire to sleep with us is also keeping us around for good.

NEVER HAVE I EVER dated a fellow redhead.

As a red, the question of "Will I ever date one of my own?" has likely cropped into your subconscious. And if you're a norm, you may have wondered about whether reds are allowed to date each other, or if their beauty simply makes them spontaneously combust upon impact. The answer, just so we're all on the same page, is that redheads do date each other. (And they aren't even combustible!) It happens all the time. In fact, there are whole dating sites dedicated to redheads meeting and potentially procreating with other reds—like dateginger.com, hotforginger.com, and findaginger.com, among others.

That being said, "Would you ever date another redhead?" is probably a question you've been asked if you're a red. And depending on your preferences, the answers vary. Brunettes certainly date each other, as do people with blond or black hair. And you'd never hear a norm brunette say, "Oh, I'd never date another brunette." But when you really think about that question,

"Would you ever date another redhead?" it seems strange that people think it's OK to ask that, doesn't it?

And yet too often we'll hear reds answer the question of whether or not they'd date someone with their own hair color with a "no." So what's the deal? The truth is that because reds are so rare, some of us avoid dating fellow reds because of the attention it would get. We already get a lot of solo attention for our hair, but if there were two reds walking down the street together hand in hand, that would likely draw even more (or possibly open up a hole in the sidewalk to another dimension). You'll also occasionally hear a red say, "It would be like dating my sibling." And to be fair to those people, their siblings might be the only other reds they've had a lot of contact with, so the associations aren't totally far-fetched.

For some reds, not dating a fellow ginger may relate to how they feel about themselves. A great example of that feeling can be seen in *Being Ginger*, a documentary about what it's like to be a redhead man. When you watch that film, you'll see that the filmmaker doesn't date redheads because he has his own self-esteem issues around his hair color. He views his hair as ugly and therefore can't bring himself to date someone with that same tinge. By the end, though, he's much more self-aware of the choices he's making and even ends up having a crush on a ginger woman. So if you have these tendencies, just know they can change over time—there are a lot of red fish in the sea, and if you're fishing as a red, there are plenty of opportunities to reel in a like-minded soul.

 NEVER HAVE I EVER been called "firecrotch."

THE BIG REDHEAD BOOK

Even if you haven't been called a firecrotch, it's best to take a sip out of solidarity for those of us who have. Because as a redhead, we woke up like this: with red pubic hair. We have it, and some fools still feel the need to ask about it. Raise your hand if a complete stranger has asked, "Does the carpet match the drapes?"

To know that there's hot sauce (or whatever else you want to nickname red pubes) on someone's body, and particularly on their nether regions, can be a confusing thing, I guess. That's really the only way to explain other people's fascination. Or perhaps it's that our pubes have an otherworldly quality that draws norms toward us, like moths to the burning flame of our bush. Now, all that being said, I'd like to suggest here and now that we take back the word "firecrotch" as a group. It's not shameful to have pubic hair—surprise: everyone has it!—and the fact that ours just happens to be the color of roses isn't a burden; it's a blessing. Sure, it's superweird that people talk about our pubes so openly, but that doesn't mean we should be ashamed of them. So go out, embrace your firecrotch, and only sleep with people who appreciate it for what it truly is: a magical thing of beauty.

REDHEAD SECRET:
Only a ginger can use the term "firecrotch."

My Red Awakening

I don't know how old most people are when they realize that they will, in fact, grow pubic hair, but I was nine. It was the summer, and my cousin Lauren was staying with us for the week. For better or worse, I looked up to her for the reason that prepubescent little girls look up to anyone: because she was pretty. At thirteen, Lauren embodied every aspect of what I wanted to be. She was thin, had straight teeth, and, thanks to the Florida sun, her skin had tanned to a buttery brown. She almost shimmered. I fell on the opposite end of the spectrum. That summer my pale skin became chalk-white from the SPF 50 I shellacked on. And my hair, which was naturally curly, morphed into frizzy lightning bolts that shot off my head from the humidity. I was an overweight ("prime for adult diabetes," as my pediatrician told me) short kid, with shiny metal braces. Which kind of answers the question of whether or not I was a popular kid in school.

Our routine during these visits tended to be wake up, eat breakfast, then spend the rest of the day by the pool. So after breakfast I waited for Lauren to finish getting ready: she put on her bikini, tied her hair in a cheerleader-esque ponytail, and proceeded to prop one leg up on the side of my bed. She then pulled out a disposable razor and quickly began to run it across her bare leg. I don't need to tell you that as an unpopular nine-year-old, I was more than a little confused.

"What, uh, what are you doing?" I asked.

"Shaving my legs," Lauren said, without pausing.

"Well, my hairs are blond," I said, thinking this might somehow make me cool. And it was true: the hair on my arms and legs was practically invisible. "I'll never have to shave."

Then I remember Lauren turning to me with the kind of maniacal grimace I'd see on my brother right before he'd give me a rug burn. "When you get older," she said, "you're going to grow red hair. Everywhere." She pointed to the bottom part of her bikini, "Even here."

I looked at her bikini, then down at my own. I was horrified. Hair . . . down WHERE? "I will not!" I shouted. I'm not totally sure why—maybe because I hadn't been given the whole puberty talk, or my tomboyish nature, or because I could tell she was trying to upset me—but, regardless, I *was* unsettled.

Throughout the rest of the day, I thought about what she'd said about growing more hair . . . down there. And the fact that it'd be red hair. I couldn't picture it. I tried to, but I couldn't imagine how the same color I had on my head would just suddenly appear on my vagina. That seemed completely bizarre, like an episode of the *X-Files*, only worse. So I did what any modern kid would: I crept into our study later that night, locked the door behind me, and typed "redhead vagina" into our computer's search engine.

Needless to say, that was the day I not only learned about pubic hair but also discovered porn. Hundreds of sites dedicated to redheads and their nether regions popped up, and like any good sleuth, I clicked on all of them. I saw what Lauren had promised—red hair down there. I felt awakened—sexually, spiritually, physically, all of the words that end with "ally." People didn't just like red pubes; they liked red hair in general. It was something to embrace and be excited by. I could see it on the sites and in the way the women weren't embarrassed of showing it off. Lauren had been so wrong. I didn't need to worry about hair growing anywhere—I would eagerly look forward to it.

And speaking from experience, it's all worked out just fine for me (and my ginger pubes).

four

PhenoMENal Red Men

Because It's Time We Start Appreciating Our Greatest Natural Resource

We all remember our first time: that magical moment when you go from being young and naive to wise and savvy. Once it happens, all you want is to have it again, and again . . . and again. (And no, that's not the first time I'm talking about, you heathens.)

For me, the first time I saw a sexy redhead man was while shopping for message tees at Urban Outfitters. I had just tried on and decided to purchase a bright orange shirt with the words ALASKA IS FOR LOVERS written across the boob portion. I am not from Alaska, nor did I actually know what those words meant, but as a seventeen-year-old, all I wanted was to look cool. So I decided to throw my money at the potential coolness and proceeded to the checkout counter. I heard "Next!" and saw that the person waving me over was one very tall drink of ginger water. He had the faintest of ginger beard shadows, there was an outline of muscles underneath his purposely tattered shirt, and his head was rich with deep wavy red hair. I wiped the drool with the back of my hand, hoping he hadn't seen. He'd only said the word "next," but I sensed that he was likely an aspiring poet/visionary/doctor or engaged in some other

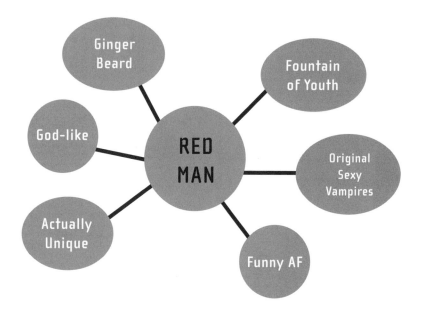

occupation worthy of him. I don't remember much of our interaction after that. I think part of my brain blacked out to prevent it from overheating. I'd like to say I got that ginger's number, offered to buy him a mansion, or told him that he was a descendant of a Greek god, but I didn't. I admired and left, fearful that security would come if I stared for much longer.

> **PRO TIP:** Don't frighten an attractive ginger man by staring for too long.

That's the very real effect that ginger men have on us: we're overwhelmed, intrigued, and borderline short-circuited in their presence. Maybe this explains why red men are treated so differently than red women—norms simply don't know how to handle all of the beauty they're seeing. And not that you need any more convincing, but redhead men are hot. Like, find-your-fainting-couch and have-a-leather-strap-to-bite-on hot. But for various reasons, which we'll go into, redhead men aren't at all appreciated the way they deserve to be. In fact, they've been systematically discriminated against solely based on their looks—stereotyped and marginalized to a point where over the past few decades it's become acceptable for norms to say they aren't attracted to men with ginger hair. Hell, there was even a sperm bank in Denmark that started turning away redhead men because of a lack of demand.[16] So we have a lot of work to do to reverse the damage done to the image of the redhead man, and that starts by understanding why ginger men are treated so differently.

FOUR *MAJOR* REASONS WHY RED MEN ARE MISUNDERSTOOD

They're EVIL

ANTI-SEMITISM

Lack of OBJECTIFICATION

Always a SIDEKICK, never a lead

> *As a kid, they assumed I was either going to be a bully or a nerd, and those were the two roles that they thought guys with red hair could play. And I just thought, "Maybe I could just be a human being like everyone else."*
>
> CAMERON MONAGHAN,
> SHAMELESS, GOTHAM, *AND MORE,*
> *IN CONVERSATION WITH ME*

Life is hard, right? Like, how are norms supposed to know what the hell to do when they see a ginge man approaching? Should they call for help or simply act like human beings?

Well, as it stands, the current sitch is this: instead of admiring the beauty of flaming red locks, norms see the color red and, like bulls charging for the cloth, promptly stomp all over it. So what are the reasons behind all this? Sure, being different means people are naturally going to wonder about you, but then how can we explain the fact that redheaded women are borderline revered, while our men end up snubbed? What could it possibly be about a hair color that polarizes men into one category (nonsexual) and women into the other (red-haired vixens)? Let's examine some of the history behind this so we can better understand the mistakes that led us all to this point.

✦ **REASON 1:** There's a weird and unfair notion that ginger men are evil. As John T. Fitzgerald, Professor of New Testament and Early Christianity at the University of Notre Dame points out, red hair has a well-worn history of being perceived as treacherous. "Red as a color sometimes has negative connotations," Dr. Fitzgerald told me. And he cited historic examples, from the Greek philosopher Polemon to the Greek physician and writer Adamantius, of how redheads have consistently been described in less than favorable lights. "According to Polemon, a face that is a little red indicates, among other things, treachery. Great redness of the face indicates lack of modesty, and a red chest indicates much anger. According to Adamantius, an entirely red body indicates a man who is deceitful and cunning. According to an anonymous Latin author, a man with thin red hair indicates a lack of manliness. In short, red sometimes (but not always) has negative connotations," Dr. Fitzgerald said.

It's not just ancient Greek sources that helped shape our image of the red man, however, because there's also the Egyptian god Set, a powerful and dangerous god, who also happened to be a ginger. He was alternately worshipped and vilified by the Egyptians. He was associated with chaos and storms, and was responsible for things like eclipses and earthquakes. He was also a bit of a bully, and part of his mythology includes a story about him killing his own brother, Osiris, and then mutilating his corpse . . . Yeah, not a supernice thing to do! Then there's the god Thor, who's now more popularly known for all things Marvel, but back in the day he was really known for his giant hammer and big red beard that shot lightning out of it. In other words, no one wanted to fuck with Thor because he could make bad things happen. So we've got a history of evil, treachery, and bullying associations with red hair. And while it may seem like a stretch to think these ancient ideas influenced how we feel about ginger men today, just look at Syndrome in *The Incredibles* and try to tell me that we aren't still holding tightly to these beliefs.

✦ **REASON 2:** Red hair is often associated with being Jewish—as many Jews are blessed with ginger locks! And some of the anti-redhead sentiments can be traced to anti-Semitism. A lot of that comes back to Judas, who was a Jew and was often portrayed as a redhead. And in medieval Europe, anti-Semitic writings and art often featured Jews with

Stewart Cook/REX/Shutterstock.com

red hair to further portray them as satanic.[17] Anti-Semitism still exists, and the portrayal of Jews as evil is easy to see through the pop culture lens. For example, the character of Magneto from the X-Men was a ginger who was originally portrayed as a Jewish Holocaust survivor and an evil character in the early iterations of the series. That image has since been toned down, and Magneto has become a more sympathetic character in more recent adaptations. Though the red hair remains: Magneto was portrayed by ginger actor Michael Fassbender in several of the recent movies.

✦ **REASON 3:** Ginger men continue to be cast as funny sidekicks and not leading men in media. Here's a challenge to illustrate my point: think

Jonathan Hordle/REX/Shutterstock.com

of a blockbuster film. Any film. Have one? OK, now try to think of a blockbuster film with a leading red man. Have one? No? That's because there are none. And yet, particularly for young and impressionable men, those are the types of films and heroes they're taught to worship. So what effect does it have on reds to know that they're not part of that conversation whatsoever? Instead, we've seen plenty of red men as the witty sidekicks, which aren't traditionally sexy roles to play. And even when love interests are introduced for those sidekicks, it's often played as part of the jokes. Just look at Danny Bonaduce on *The Partridge Family* and Seth Green in practically every role he's ever played (Kenny in *Can't Hardly Wait*, Oz in *Buffy*, and Jared in *Broad City*). Then there's Rupert Grint, an undeniable icon as Ron Weasley in the Harry Potter series

> In Hollywood I constantly have agents, producers, TV networks, film studios, and movie people say to my agent, "It's too bad he's a redhead, he's perfect for the role! But we can't sell a redhead lead, so we're not going to cast him."
>
> —ACTOR AND MODEL DANIEL NEWMAN, THE WALKING DEAD, SEX AND THE CITY, AND THE VAMPIRE DIARIES, AMONG OTHER THINGS, IN CONVERSATION WITH ME

who also winds up with Hermione Granger by his side. And while that's at least thirty Quidditch points for reds everywhere, when we actually look at their relationship, it was Ron who existed as the bumbling, awkward one, while his partner, Hermione, was seen as the fearless genius. See what I'm saying? Yes, red men are hilarious, but that's not all they are. And since the roles they've primarily been cast in err on the side of bumbling funny guy, it can have the effect of desexualizing our hot men.

♦ *REASON 4:* There's been an unforgivable lack of objectification of ginger men in the media. I mean, how often do you see red men shirtless and giving come-hither looks? Almost never. And there just aren't enough sex scenes to get the blood pumping here, but when there *are* sex scenes it's nothing short of beautiful—just remember Robert Redford in *The Way We Were*, Kevin McKidd in *Grey's Anatomy*, and Prince Harry in all of your illicit fantasies. Even when red men do get their time to shine—like when *Twilight* was published and Edward was described as a redhead ("Which one is the boy with the reddish-brown hair?" Bella asks in the book)—the media will snatch it from them and cast a person who's not even close to being a ginger. (Not that Robert Pattinson isn't a gorgeous man, but come on!) So Hollywood's belief that redheaded men can't be sex symbols then becomes a self-fulfilling prophecy for actual ginger men. They sense that audiences don't view them as sexual, and they therefore don't feel sexual. Likewise, as an audience, we assume ginger men aren't meant to be desired because we aren't shown them in that context. It's a damn vicious cycle.

Redhead men have only been marketed and sold to the mainstream public in film and TV as the villains, the ugly outcasts, mean, violent, or in comedies as the punchline, the bad date, the joke, or more recently as the "cute friend," the lovable, sweet, quirky boy, the sensitive artist, etc. But never the hot young heartthrob leading man. Never a Brad Pitt image. Only the mean pissed-off cop that arrests Brad Pitt.

ACTOR AND MODEL
DANIEL NEWMAN

THINGS ARE GETTING REDDER, THOUGH

We've spent some time dwelling on how we got to the place of red men not being worshipped, but now it's time to readjust our focus and zero in on the cold hard facts: things are getting redder. For so long the ideal of male beauty has involved the phrase "tall, dark, and handsome." But as anyone who is a red man or has seen one before knows, the more accurate description is "tall, red, and handsome." When you look at a red man, much like with his female counterpart, it's like walking through the wardrobe and straight into Narnia. They transport you to a place where everything is enchanting. It's because they're incredibly striking; you can't miss them in a crowd, and more likely than not, people's heads will turn to see them.

You just need to watch *Outlander* on Starz and check out the hair on male lead, Jamie Fraser, to see what I mean. It's a color that leads Claire, his wife, to say, "It really was the most extraordinary mop of red you've ever seen." (Admittedly, actor Sam Heughan is a natural brunette, but we've gotta start somewhere.) And the character Jamie Fraser is explicitly sexual; he's strong, take-charge, and not at all shy of going after what he wants in the bedroom. And Damian Lewis, a real ginger, starred in *Homeland* as a terribly hot and terribly disturbed former U.S. marine. His character was complex, and at times you didn't know whether to root for him or hate him, but there was nothing "sidekick" about Agent Brody. So there are more roles for our red men, and the roles are becoming much more diverse than they were before.

But since our history is so rooted in art, it's just as important to highlight Thomas Knights's *Red Hot* photography project, which is a celebration of all things ginger male. In 2013, Knights, a London-based photographer and fellow redhead, decided that ginger men were being underappreciated. He didn't see them portrayed as sex symbols in media, and instead saw the bullying that is too often directed at them. "I noticed growing up that it was very negative to be a ginger guy," Knights told me. "More than anything it struck me that there was this real imbalance in the gender. I thought, if it's OK to be a redhead woman that can be inspiring and held in the highest regard and overtly sexualized—a very powerful figure—then what happened with the men? Where did that go wrong? And it just got me thinking about it." To combat the views held about ginger men, he created *Red Hot*, a photography exhibit which featured 160 ginger men in poses and stances that asserted their sexual prowess. These men are pictured shirtless, eye-fucking the camera, and flaunting their beautiful heads of red hair. If you look at the photos and aren't

Thomas Knights

> *I don't think people take it very seriously, the discrimination against redheads. It's very easy for people to laugh about it because it's your hair color, but actually it's an innate part of who you are and if you're being put down for it every day, it's going to have this big impact on you.*
>
> PHOTOGRAPHER THOMAS KNIGHTS

profusely sweating, then you're doing your life wrong. "We had people coming into the exhibition saying they had no idea that you could get good-looking ginger men," Knights said. "They were just dumbfounded that they even existed, which was so wrong but also great."

That people didn't know hot redhead men existed highlights how deep prejudice against redhead males runs. Which is unfortunate, especially given what a gift they are to this world. Knights describes the *Red Hot* exhibition as photography that turned into a kind of advertising project. He saw that having these redheaded men pose in confident, heroic, and sexually charged ways changed the models' perception of themselves, and also the tone of how redheads were discussed at large. Through his magazine-style imagery, Knights was able to change the conversation about redheads from negative to positive. "A lot of the redheads I've talked to have noticed a really remarkable change in their general attractiveness, and their stake went up after the project got a lot of traction," Knights said.

Luckily the impact of *Red Hot* was felt, and because of the striking images and the men in them, the exhibit went viral—getting coverage in places like *Slate, Huffington Post, Daily Mail,* and *The New York Times,* among others. "The time was right for it," Knights said, citing the buzz around men like Prince Harry and Damian Lewis as helpful in the spread of his positive photography.

The spread of positive depictions of redheaded men through social media, like Knights's photos, leads to norms and reds alike viewing ginger men differently. Many of the models in *Red Hot* have gone on to model for brands like Mulberry, Esprit, Fashion Revolution, and People Tree. Which means that an even larger audience gets to see these red-hot reds in a sexually charged light. We're seeing depictions that break the old stereotypes down and invent some new ones. Like the new stereotype that shirtless redhead men are hotter than other men . . .

SCIENTIFICALLY PROVEN REASONS RED MEN > ALL MEN

Just so we're all on the same crimson-clear page here: by "scientifically," I of course mean observational science. And by "science," I of course mean my strongly held beliefs. But that's only because no studies have been done on the phenomenon that is ginger men being better than most other men. If the science community threw a little money behind this, I'd have cold hard data to back me up. But for now, let's stick to what we know in our gut: ginger men are the best kind of men. And we have plenty of reasons to assert this claim.

Ginger beards are their own form of foreplay. As we learned earlier, just seeing the color red can make our heart rate increase. So staring into a full ginger beard is going to make you impossibly parched.

REDHEAD SECRET:
A ginger beard is the only thing a red man needs to wear. Ever.

Gingers are uncommon, like a glass of Pappy Van Winkle (a really rare and delicious whiskey only a few get the pleasure of tasting). So if you happen to nab one, it means they've deemed you worthy of appreciating their beauty. Some people will have to go their entire existence without ever experiencing a ginger man—pray for those people and their sad lives.

Since ginger men are teased so much as kids, they develop a strong personality to survive. Unlike most norms, ginger men are sent through a Dumpster fire of a journey when it comes to puberty. It's like normal puberty, but also like having someone kick you in the balls on a daily basis. Because of this they often have to develop actual personalities, which in turn makes them better humans later in life.

This one's not up for debate: red men don't realize how hot they are. It's like ugly-duckling syndrome. They're truly gorgeous, but constantly think they're not worthy. Which means when you date a ginger man you get to reap the benefits of a humble but infinitely hot person.

Redhead men know to avoid the sun. So while the rest of the men become middle aged and shrivel up like sad little walnuts, our ginger men will age at a much slower rate. Kind of like a sparkly vampire but, ya know, without the blood-sucking aspect.

Is your current mood "sick of dating men who are basically lukewarm glasses of milk"? Great, then you're an actual human being and you deserve a ginger man who won't look like all of the other generic dudes you see on a day-to-day basis.

And according to ancient ginger legend, if you manage to count all the freckles on a redhead man's body, you'll live forever. This is 100 percent accurate. Don't ask questions.

ACCEPTABLE PICKUP LINES TO USE ON GINGER MEN

1. "Are you from the ocean? Because I didn't realize Ariel had a twin brother."
2. "If you ever do feel fiery, I wouldn't try to extinguish those flames."
3. "I don't believe any of those redhead stereotypes. Except now I know the one about all redheads being hot is true."
4. "Do people just assume you're a model because you look like a rare bird of paradise?"

SMOKING *HOT GINGER FILL-IN-THE-BLANK*

Think you're a sexy-red-man pro now? Well, in that case, let's see what kind of

fanfic you can weave by filling this bad boy out.

I met _____ (PROPER NOUN), the most beautiful ginger

man I'd ever laid eyes on, when I accidentally walked in a room only to find

him _____ (VERB) in a _____ (NOUN). I was _____

(ADJECTIVE), and exhaled sharply. He turned, and I tried not to stare at his

_____ (NOUN). I can't say I was surprised, I knew redhead men were

_____ (ADJECTIVE). "Sorry," he smiled. "I didn't know anyone would

be in here. Should I leave?"

I _____ (VERB) and said, "No, why don't you _____

(VERB)?"

"I'd be happy to," he said.

That was five years ago. And we meet every _____ (DATE) to

_____ (VERB). It's true what they say: Once you go red, you'll never

_____ (PHRASE).

five

Redhead Beauty Basics

Facts, Tips, and Brushstrokes About Beauty as a Red

Sephora is a magical place, like the Disneyland of makeup stores. And for most people, stepping in and eyeballing the sections is like trying to choose which ride to go on first—damn near impossible. But for redheads, the makeup process is even more complicated. Not only do we have to navigate the Disneyland that is finding the perfect makeup, but we also live in a makeup world that wasn't made for us. Our hair color alone throws a wrench into the color palette, and if you're a red who also happens to have freckles or impossibly fair skin, then the quest just gets ever more precarious. The questions redheads have when in a makeup store aren't so much, "Which bronzer should I buy?" but more like, "Which bronzer won't simultaneously make it look like I am one giant freckle?"

So in an effort to save my fellow reds time and energy, this chapter will serve as your ginger stylist and makeup BFF. For so long we've gone without the help that everyone needs when figuring out their own style, but from here on out, this chapter has got your back. Redheads have to stick together, and if we can't meet to discuss these things IRL, then let this book serve as a way to put everything on the table.

Time Spent at Sephora (hours)

8 — 7 — 6 — 5 — 4 — 3 — 2 — 1

1 2 3 4 5 6 7 8 9 10

Level of Happiness

brunettes
black-haired
blondes
redheads

THE BIG REDHEAD BOOK

A FEW REMINDERS ABOUT **REDHEAD** BEAUTY

People often make the mistake of grouping all redheads into one gorgeous clump because they assume we all look alike. "Has anyone ever told you that you look like [insert famous redhead here]?" is a common question for a red to get asked. Even if you don't look like that person whatsoever aside from the hair color. Hell, it even happens to famous reds like Jessica Chastain and Bryce Dallas Howard, two very beautiful and very different people who get mistaken for each other on a regular basis. It happens so much, in fact, that Howard sang a song called, "I Am Not Jessica Chastain" for an Instagram video.[18]

And the "redheads all look alike" phenomenon is just one thing that the norms get wrong about us. So just to make sure we're all on the same red page here, let's get a few things straight about redheads and the way we look (or, rather, the way other people think we look):

Allow me to blow your mind: redheads aren't only white, fair-skinned people. Red hair isn't exclusive to one race. There's even a Hawaiian word for Polynesians with red hair, *'ehu* or *ha 'ehu 'ehu*, and Polynesians believe the *'ehu* are descendants from the fire gods.[19] (Personally, I think all reds are descendants of gods, but that's just my theory.) The idea that redheads are all white even led to the creation of a photography project called *The MC1R Series,* by Michelle Marshall. Marshall is trying to photograph redheads within black and mixed-race communities so she can help dispel these myths. So hopefully we're all on the same page now: #notallredheads.

Are you sitting down? Because not all redheads have freckles. As we know, freckles are tiny reminders that we're one of the gods' chosen people, but not all redheads have them. Freckles are caused by the *MC1R* gene, and in general, that gene controls our red hair color and the freckles we have on our skin. But variations of that *MC1R* gene will determine how many freckles we end up having, if any.

Break out the confetti, because we can also have any kind of eye color. The rarest hair and eye color combination in the world is red hair with blue eyes. So if you're one of those people, just know you're as rare as a super blood moon eclipse.

And finally, hear me when I say this: our hair color has a wide spectrum. People often associate red hair with the bright copper tone. But red comes in so many varieties: even that coppery tone has a spectrum from light copper to deep copper. And we run the range from strawberry blond all the way to a deep wine shade. So don't make the mistake of limiting us to one color wheel, because we'll break that wheel apart and send it flying back at you.

In some ways my red hair has been a way into the world because people comment on it. A lot of times I'll get into an elevator and someone will say "pretty hair," or it'll be like, "my sister has that color hair."

ACTRESS MARIA THAYER,
FORGETTING SARAH MARSHALL,
ACCEPTED, *AND* STRANGERS WITH CANDY,
IN CONVERSATION WITH ME

OUR HAIR

This is a book about red hair, and to not gush over it as often as possible is like asking sweet grandparents to stop showing off photos of their grandkids (and nobody is going to do that). Our hair is what frames our face, creating a ring of fire around our mouth, eyes, and nose. And it has psychological affects on the person looking at us. If you have a deep red, when another person sees that color it increases their heart rate, blood pressure, and even metabolism. In general, a deeper red is associated with danger, blood, courage, power, and lust, which means if you have that color you're associated with those things too (in other people's minds, at the very least). While a more orange color is psychologically associated with warmth, happiness, creativity, and determination. See what I mean? No way could we skip more hair talk.

OUR FRECKLES

Not all redheads freckle, but those who do often have a helluva time coming to terms with just how beautiful their freckles can be. But when you do allow your skin to be its sun-kissed self, you'll come to realize that what you were hiding were marks that are completely and utterly your own. No one else's freckles are exactly like yours, which makes you kind of like a snowflake.

OUR SKIN

Maybe you're a tan red. Or a person of color with red hair. Or pale with a tinge of ginge. But regardless, you get an extra boost from being a redhead. That's because regardless of skin tone, when our hair frames our face it allows us to glow even more than we naturally do—like a fiery halo. And more often than not, our skin simply looks different than everyone else's. Even people who have similar coloring to ours don't have quite the same tones as we do. The skin tone of the redhead drives us to find exactly the right shades of makeup or pick clothing based on what helps us shine and not get washed out.

OUR CONFIDENCE

When we walk into a room, people turn to look, and as a result we have an inner poise that's impossible to replicate. This only grows when we meet fellow reds or get acknowledged by them out in the wild. So by the time we've come to love and appreciate everything about our hair (typically in our twenties), we also view ourselves as spectacular. And, as we all know, there's nothing quite as attractive as someone with confidence.

How I Learned to Love My Freckles

I don't think anyone would tell a freckly person, "cover those up," to their face—and if they did, they'd be enormous dinguses—but I've certainly learned that freckles aren't the ideal through what I've seen in media. Which, to be blunt, are very few freckles. And when I have gotten my makeup done at a makeup counter, there's always one consistent thing the artists do: cover my freckles with foundation. So up until my late twenties I spent a good chunk of each morning slathering my face with heavy foundation. All the hours I squandered painting my face like a ceramic bowl could probably have added up to my being a musical prodigy. And, let me tell you, few things are sexier than a ceramic bowl, right?

On my twenty-ninth birthday, however, I realized that I hadn't gone a single day since I was twelve years old without wearing makeup. That's seventeen years of makeup, not unlike a prison term. There's nothing wrong with makeup—it's empowering and, much like a new outfit, can make you feel fiercer in your everyday life. But what I didn't love was that the idea of not wearing makeup scared me. My face and no makeup? No thank you. I didn't want strangers to be able to see that, call the cops, and have me arrested for walking with the intent to show my real self. And I wasn't about to let the people I deeply cared about, like my boyfriend, see me. And that made me sad, the kind of sad that can only be fixed by eating a pound of chocolate and actually doing something about it. So I challenged myself to go for a week without any makeup. No foundation, no concealer, no loose powder to cover me up—it would just be me, myself, and my bare face. I was fucking terrified. I didn't want to do it. That first morning, I almost

chickened out and picked up my close friend, the foundation brush. But then I remembered that me without makeup deserved a real shot.

I went through the first day hating myself and how I looked when I caught a glimpse in a mirror. I thought about calling in sick from work. I could stay home, where at least my cat wouldn't be able to judge me (or, if she did judge, she wouldn't be able to tell me). The thing is, no one was judging me. I was judging me. I was basing my desire for a clear complexion on what I saw in the media—freckle-free faces. It was really silly, now that I think back on it. But that's what media pressure can do: turn you into an idiot most of the time.

On the fourth day, I let my boyfriend see me—the whole me—sans makeup. I was so self-conscious that I lit a bunch of candles instead of turning on actual lights. "Mood lighting," I told him, and casually draped a scarf around my face. He didn't say anything. So I blurted out, "I'm not wearing makeup this week." "You aren't?" he said, and paused. "You look really beautiful without it. Maybe you shouldn't wear it anymore." (A) What a great boyfriend (I eventually married him, because he's so great), and (B) that was really all I needed to hear. I just wanted to know that I still resembled myself.

It wasn't until the last day of my challenge that I really looked in the mirror. Up until that point I'd glance, not spending too much time focusing on myself because I was afraid of what I'd see there. Maybe looking into the mirror would crack it, or open a portal to a place where all of the makeup-free women are forced to go. It was a new and startling time for me. But when I did examine myself closely, I realized that I hadn't paid much attention to my freckles in a long time. I'd spent all those years trying to erase them so that I forgot they were there altogether—on my nose, my cheeks, forehead, and just above my lip. Little golden marks of warmth. I surprised myself, in that I thought they looked fine, and more than fine, kinda precious even. Had I been missing this all along? Was I

Continued on next page

Continued from previous page

so afraid of being different that I couldn't even see that those distinctive marks were actually cute?

The no-makeup week passed, but I decided to permanently lay off the foundation. Fuck foundation, right?! I wanted to see what my newly discovered freckles could do. Like, I found that they made my nose look completely different than it did with makeup—a little sun-kissed, a little more distinguished because of the shadows the freckles seemed to cast. And I liked how they framed my lips, almost acting like a lip liner. Every day that I allowed them breathing room, I realized that I'd been missing out on this very real and special part of my redheadedness. They changed how I appeared, but not in the bad way I thought they would: 10/10 would go makeup-free again.

FACTS ABOUT *RED* STYLE

REDHEAD SECRET:
You can't spell "dress" without "red."

To paraphrase Harry Winston, if people are going to stare, you might as well make it worth their while. Such is the argument I make to you, my fellow reds. And I know this is a tough one because as a red, more often than not we're told what we shouldn't wear instead of what we should wear. People seem to have a lot of ideas about what looks great on redheads and what should be locked in an underground safe. But why are we letting other people decide what's best for us? Let's banish some old and tired thoughts and bring in new ideas for how to stock your closet. In other words: make it worth their while.

FACT: There Are Colors Redheads Should Always Wear

Contrary to what some ill-advised salespeople may have whispered in your ear, green, red, and yellow, are exceptionally complementary color choices for us reds. Shades of blue, pink, and violet can also be fresh as hell when you're figuring out what to wear. And Adrienne and Stephanie Vendetti, cofounders of the beauty site *How to Be a Redhead*, are huge fans of emerald, plum, ruby, cranberry, and mustard on all redheads of any shade. "If you're going to take a risk and wear something out of your box, or you think won't look good with your red hair, tame it down on your eye makeup, and do a simple lip gloss and you should be good to go," Stephanie told me.

FACT: Norms Think There Are Colors Reds Should Avoid

White, yellow, and red are colors that other people will often suggest redheads avoid. White allegedly washes us out, yellow makes us appear seasick, and red on red is a fashion hellscape, according to these alleged experts. But the crazy thing is that those opinions are just unfounded. According to *How to Be a Redhead*, a piece of red clothing, especially if it's a scarlet red, looks incredible with our strands—just google "Julianne Moore red dress" if you don't believe me. Also, just do that anyway because it's superfun. And yellows and whites can totally be pulled off,

David Fisher/REX/Shutterstock.com

especially if your makeup is a bit more intense against the less bright tones. Layering those neutral colors with brighter tones (like a white dress with a cerulean blue jacket) can really pull everything together too. So as for what colors reds should avoid, the answer is none.

 ## FACT: Accessories Highlight Your Hair

Mirror, mirror, on the wall, our red tresses are the fairest of them all. And, as such, we need accessories to draw even more attention to our locks, skin, and freckles—all the things we should readily emphasize. A sparkly headband, cute clip, or a flower crown if you're feeling flashy will only bring more eyes to that hair. And even though your red is its own pop of color, don't be afraid to go loud with the color of your accessories. Emerald green, violet, and fuchsia should all be on the accessories table. Keep those colors in mind if you want to add a strong necklace as an accessory. What better way to draw attention to your neck and collarbones (and, in turn, that beautiful skin) than with a necklace to draw the eye in? If you're a ginger lad, a hat will cover some of your hair but also add a nice contrast to it. And a leather bracelet or a chunky watch draws the eye to that ginger skin in the best way possible.

FACT: Reds Have Better Style Icons

Katharine Hepburn: From *The Philadelphia Story* to *Lion in Winter*, this redhead became an icon because of her androgynous look; she was all about trousers, blazers, and collared shirts. She was also incredibly opinionated about her style and gave elaborate feedback on everything from the color to the concept of the clothes she'd be seen in on film.

Molly Ringwald: Inspirational doesn't even really encompass the effect Ringwald had on the '80s. I mean, yes, her films are all must-sees (*The Breakfast Club* is my personal fave). But if Molly taught reds anything, it's that we definitely look pretty in pink (see what I did there?) and not to be afraid of pastels. She was kind of a pro at mixing feminine details with masculine ones, and girl knew how to work accessories that emphasized that red—oversized glasses and bowler hats are always welcome.

StarTraks/REX/
Shutterstock.com

Grace Coddington: If you want to know the real creative genius behind *Vogue*, it's Grace Coddington, who serves as the magazine's creative director. Because of Grace's personal style, which bled into the direction of the magazine, we know that bold colors are the right choice for reds, and there's nothing wrong with a wild pattern either.

Farrell/BFA/REX/
Shutterstock.com

Jessica Chastain: This ginger is pretty new to the scene, as she only came onto our screens in 2011 with *The Help*. But chic is pretty much the word that sums her up—clean silhouettes, classic colors, and elegant details. And when you put beautiful redheads into sleek designs, they take on a regal quality. So if you want to seem like royalty, model your own style after our ginger princess, Jessica.

Curtis/Starfix/REX/
Shutterstock.com

Ewan McGregor: This *Star Wars* star is a golden ginger in that his hair looks exceptionally red in the sunlight and turns a deep auburn indoors. And likewise, his style can be just as versatile. When he's out and about it's best described as biker chic, with lots of leather jackets, striped shirts, and dark pants. And when it comes time to clean up, he takes that alternative biker style and applies it to his formal wear. So if you're a ginger who needs a little edge, Ewan is the man to emulate.

REX/Shutterstock.com

Damian Lewis: This man can wear a suit. What Jessica Chastain is to chic female-red style, Damian Lewis is to male fashion. Unlike his *Homeland* character, IRL Lewis rocks long trench coats, shiny suits, crushed velvet jackets, and corduroy pants, and makes them all seem expensive and tailored. So if you ever want to cop this style, stay well groomed and don't be afraid of a dark suit jacket.

PicturePerfect/REX/Shutterstock.com

Geri "Ginger Spice" Halliwell: Her Union Jack dress at the 1997 Brit Awards is not just the outfit Ginger Spice is remembered for, it's one of the most iconic dresses of all time. The supermini was originally all black, but Geri asked her sister to sew on a Union Jack tea towel to the front to celebrate being British. To prove how iconic this was, the dress sold in 1998 for 41,320 pounds and now holds the Guinness World Record for being the most expensive piece of clothing worn by a popstar ever sold at auction.

Jonathan Hordle/REX/Shutterstock.com

Rihanna: Remember Rihanna's red phase? Or, as I like to call it, her best fashion decision thus far? If you need more proof, google her 2011 *Vogue* cover. That cover photo truly popped because of her bright red hair. She was styled (in my mind) like Ariel in *The Little Mermaid*, and her sheer beaded Chanel dress made it look like she'd just swum out of the ocean and into the photoshoot. She's no natural redhead, but maybe she should've been born one?

Curtis/Starfix/REX/Shutterstock.com

COSTUME INSPIRATION FOR ADULT REDS

SOLO COSTUMES:

- Florence of Florence and the Machine
- Ginny Weasley from the Harry Potter series
- Poison Ivy
- Angela Chase from *My So-Called Life*
- Ms. Frizzle
- Dexter

COUPLE COSTUMES:

- Ygritte and Jon Snow from *Game of Thrones*
- Mitch and Cam from *Modern Family*
- Jessica Rabbit and Roger Rabbit (especially if your partner is also a ginger)
- Archie and Betty (or Veronica, or Jughead, or any of them, really)
- Joan Holloway and Don Draper from *Mad Men*
- Jean Grey and Storm from the X-Men series

WHAT TO KNOW ABOUT *MAKEUP* FOR REDS

Houston, redheads have a problem. Because while there are loads of us who like to play in the world of blushes and bronzers, the truth is that finding makeup as a redhead can feel like being lost in space. (I'm guessing.)

So think of this section as the fairy godmother of makeup you've always wanted but never had. Because as all redheads know, the agony of going to a makeup counter and dealing with an artist who's clearly never worked with reds is real. And getting a makeover only to realize they had no idea what to do with you is way too common. So let's end the pain and suffering of makeup and bring out the magical wand to wipe away all of that beauty-counter anxiety.

HOW EASILY WILL YOU FIND MAKEUP?

WHAT COLOR IS YOUR HAIR?

RED   **ANY OTHER COLOR**

100% NO PROB

CALL FOR BACKUP

Easy Makeup Know-How for Gingers

FINDING THE RIGHT RED LIPSTICK: I'll fill you in on a big red secret: red lipstick is hot AF on us. But before you buy, consider what kind of a finish you want. If you're looking for something light (maybe for daytime), tinted balms as well as sheer and satin lipsticks will provide a lightweight finish. While you might opt for a matte if you plan to wear your shade at night, since the color will be deeper and need to be touched up much less. Just keep in mind that mattes and other long-wear lipsticks are more drying, so if you're prone to chapped lips, avoid those.

> For some reason there are so many perceptions about what redheads are supposed to do. It's just that you have to make sure everything is balanced, that's the hard part.
>
> ADRIENNE VENDETTI,
> HOW TO BE A REDHEAD

Unfortunately, there's no lip shade that is universally great on all reds, because our coloring varies. But figure out whether you want a warm or a cool red. Warm shades of red have more orange and yellow tints, while cool reds tend to have more purple and blues. To suss out what you like, ask a salesperson to put a sample of a warm and a cool shade on the back of your hand, and see if one of those shades screams "FIERCE, YAS" to you. And above all, try on a lot of shades of red. Have people pick some, try on the ones you spot, and pretend that you're in your own book called *Fifty Shades of Red*. It'll be just like that other book, except not at all. But at least you'll leave with a dope hue.

NAIL A NEUTRAL LIP: Regardless of what color your skin is, a good nude lip can be a great beauty trick, especially if you're trying to capture that minimal-makeup look. And it's definitely a look reds can get behind (hell, our queen, Julianne Moore, even has her own shade of nude with L'Oréal Paris called Julianne's Nude). If your skin has more pink tones, then a barely peach color (much like Julianne's shade) is the perfect way to achieve the nude look. Whereas if your skin has more blue undertones, then a shade of pink should be where you start.

LET YOUR FRECKLES SHOW: First of all, it's important to remember that some people can't even get freckles. (Praying for you, freckleless friends.) And people want them so desperately that there's recently been a makeup trend of fake tattooed freckles for those who can't be blessed with golden sun marks. Yes, tattooed freckles. Because this is the world we live in now. So instead of hiding your natural beauty, wear makeup that enhances it.

Let's start with the foundation of any makeup kit: foundation. When you buy foundation, aim for a color that matches your skin tone and not one that matches your freckles. The goal is to blend to your tone and not cover up those little sun-touched spots. Sheer-to-light coverage options include mineral powders and tinted moisturizers, which will provide a veil that doesn't overpower. And before applying foundation, put on an illuminating primer so that your makeup goes on as evenly as possible.

Another common mistake that reds make is to buy bronzer and blushes that match the color of their freckles. But then, my flawless friends, it leaves your cheeks like one massive freckle. And while that's certainly an interesting look, the better approach is to buy shades of peach and coral, which should complement and not work against those awesome freckles.

LIVE YOUR BEST EYEBROW LIFE: Eyebrows are so crucial. How else will someone know whether or not you're throwing side-eye?! And while some reds have naturally dark brows, others are fair and almost blond in color. So for the blond brows out there, get your best side-eye game with these killer options:

- Eyebrow pencil. This is easy to apply; it'll feel like shading in a drawing and has a clean finish. Scan for colors like light brown, ash blond, and auburn—you can even mix colors to get exactly the right shade for you.

- Brow powder. Much like an eyebrow pencil, a powder feels a lot like painting in part of a canvas. The only difference is that it's a soft powder instead of the hard pencil. It can be applied with a dry or damp brush, and you'll want to start by shaping the brows with a brow brush, then applying from the corner of your brow closest to your nose and sweeping out with the brush toward the outer edge of the brow. Aim for colors like ash blond, auburn, medium brown, and taupe.

- Eyebrow gel. A clear eyebrow gel can be especially useful for reds who are coloring their brows with pencil or powder. The gel will help set the color and make sure nothing comes between you and your brow perfection.

- Eyebrow tinting. Tinting is a really incredible option for reds. Much like dyeing your locks, an eyebrow tint is a semipermanent color solution that lasts anywhere from three to six weeks, and it only takes ten minutes to apply. When you go for a tint, aim for a medium- to light-brown shade, so that the color starts a little darker and has time to fade and retain on your brows.

HOW TO MAINTAIN *FLAWLESS* SKIN

For most redheads, the sun is our ultimate complicated relationship. We need less of it than other people, since we're pros at making vitamin D, but we're human beings so going outside once and a while is nice. When we do go outside, though, we have to view the sun as if it's coming at us with a light saber and put up all of our shields in the form of SPF and sun hats. As we all likely found out in grade school, our skin is the biggest organ in our body, so it's important to know how to take care of it. Especially for redheads, since the *MC1R* gene not only gives us our gorgeous mops but also makes it easier for us to get things like sunburns, which can eventually lead to skin cancer. Let's protect our complexions and learn the basics of how to be a redhead without turning into leather handbags.

WHAT'S ON MY BATHROOM COUNTER

Sunscreen

Other

Guarding Against Our Frenemy, the Sun

If you're like me, then you know the struggle of walking out your door, going for a quick five- to ten-minute jaunt, and coming back only to realize you've burnt the living hell out of every exposed bit of skin. Hmm . . . maybe we are vampires after all. But regardless: sunburns are real, and no matter how sensitive you are, we redheads need to learn how to properly protect our skin so we don't end up looking like scorched apples (or even worse, developing skin cancer, which redheads are highly prone to[20]). Luckily, there's more than just sunscreen to help us do that:

 Wear UPF (Ultraviolet Protection Factor) clothing, which you can find online and at major active-wear retailers. Basically, when you put on a piece of clothing that has UPF it's like wearing an SPF shirt. Because it's been tested to make sure the fabric blocks harmful UV rays. So when you see a piece of clothing that says UPF 50, it's extremely similar to having an SPF 50 on your body. And while you might be wondering what the difference is between a regular cotton shirt and a UPF shirt, just keep in mind that most normal shirt blends rank below SPF 30 in protection. So, yeah, a few UPF pieces to wear when you know you'll be out in the sun all day are clutch.

Wear a hat, and choose a wide-brimmed and finely woven one. If you can see through the hat, so can the sun, and the sun will get through those loosely woven spots. While hats don't provide a huge SPF benefit (about an SPF of 10), the more help you can get shading your face, the better!

 Buy cool sunglasses. And then make sure those shades have at least 90 percent UV protection.

 If you have a car, then add a UV film to your windows. This is such an easy way to protect yourself, especially if you have long commutes. You can take your ride into a dealer and ask them to add a UVA-protecting film to your windows. Head to the Skin Cancer Foundation site to see a list of approved dealers.

 Download a UV meter app. That way if you're thinking of going outside, you can gauge the best times to do so and have the least amount of possible harmful UV rays coming your way.

 And of course, the all-too-obvious one: wear sunscreen. There are so many different types—sheer, mineral, moisturizing, spray-on, lotions—and there's no excuse not to take the extra few minutes to apply. Aim for SPF 30 or higher, and reapply every hour.

The Art of the Self-Tan

I use the word "art" because to self-tan is to paint yourself like a canvas, and I do mean paint, because you'll have to coat the stuff on. But it's also the best option if you're a redhead and want to try a more bronzed approach.

Self-tanners come in a few variations, including lotion, mousse, and gel. If you're a newb, stick to a lotion that has a slight color guide to it, so you can see where you've applied and any spots you've missed. And if you've got that super pale, almost translucent skin, opt for a gradual tanning lotion. That way you'll build up color slowly and won't have to deal with being twelve shades too dark after one application. If you've been there, done that with lotions, try a gel, which goes on smoothly and is perfect for anyone with normal-to-oily skin. Only use a mousse if you're a self-tanning pro, as they dry very quickly and you can easily miss spots. And regardless of which option you choose, make sure to exfoliate your skin beforehand to nix any dead skin cells that will flake your new tanner off.

Visiting a Dermatologist Like a Pro (Something All Reds Should Do!)

An apple a day keeps the doctor away, but if you're a ginger, you just have to ignore that and go to the damn dermatologist at least once a year for a scan of your skin. Redheads are at greater risk not only for burns but also for skin cancers. And while skin cancer is the most common cancer of all, there are numerous ways to treat and prevent it. A trip to your dermatologist once or twice a year means you have a doctor inspecting your skin, freckles, and moles to make sure there's nothing suspicious to worry about. If they happen to catch something, that's the good news—they can catch it early, remove the abnormality, and it won't develop into cancer. It's all about making the appointment. Before you go, there are a few things to keep in mind:

✦ Share any family history of skin cancer. That means texting the hell out of your fam to see if they know of any skin cancer scares or issues in the past.

✦ Don't be surprised when they check just about every spot on your body, including in between your toes, behind your ears, on your scalp, and even your nail beds. This doc will know you better than you know yourself!

✦ Keep those hands busy and inspect your own skin regularly. Learn the Skin Cancer Foundation's ABCDEs so you know what to look for—if a spot is (a) asymmetrical, (b) has a misshaped border, (c) is unevenly colored, (d) seems larger than a pencil eraser in diameter, or (e) begins to evolve in the way it looks, that's something to point out to your dermatologist.

QUESTIONS TO ASK YOUR DOC

1. What kind of sun protection would you recommend?
2. Do you have any tips for doing self exams?
3. If I'm checking my skin, when should I really be worried?
4. As a redhead, how often should I come in for a skin scan?

HAIR CARE FOR REDS

I know what you're thinking: can't I just shampoo, condition, eat some fries, and call it a day? Sure, you can do that. But you can also upgrade your life and hair with some pretty simple steps. I'm talking about increasing the shine, vibrancy, and keeping those locks safe during the summer. Come on, let's do this stuff together and then top it all off with celebratory fries. Several of these ideas, and many more redhead tips, can be found at *How to Be a Redhead*—check it out!

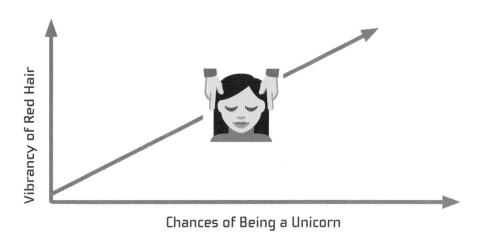

Vibrancy of Red Hair

Chances of Being a Unicorn

Keep Your Red Hair Happy

Be a nice person to your hair and buy sulfate-free shampoo. And if you're a redhead with sensitive skin, this one is particularly useful, because while sulfates give shampoo that lather we're all used to, they can also irritate your skin and cause frizziness and dull any color treatments you may have. Yeah, ban sulfates, basically.

Go glossy: ask your salon for a hair gloss to make your red more vibrant. This is an easy trick for any strawberry blondes who want to add more red, or for those whose hair gets a little faded from the summer sun. A gloss is usually applied for fifteen minutes, rinsed out, and then you're on your way to much redder tresses.

Spend a little extra dough on a color-depositing shampoo (just make sure it's sulfate-free!). Much like a gloss, this adds in more color without having to go to a salon to get a dye job.

For those times when you want to play stay-at-home spa, try a cinnamon leave-in mask. This will lighten your red and make it a little brighter (if you're into that kind of thing). To start, shampoo your hair as you normally would, then towel dry. Grab your conditioner and mix a teaspoon of cinnamon into it, then apply it from the roots to the ends while your hair is still damp. Brush through your hair a few times, then put it into a bun and leave the mixture in for six to eight hours. Rinse it out when you're down, and voilà—lightened locks!

HOW TO RESPOND IF A STRANGER ASKS, "IS THAT YOUR NATURAL COLOR?"

1. Is that how you talk to people when you want them to actually answer?

2. Are you naturally so rude?

3. Is there a delete button for that question?

4. What app do I download to make you disappear?

5. Go ahead, ask me how badly I want to walk away right now.

6. Your mom just texted; she wants to remind you not to be a jackass.

For All the Fake Reds

Maybe she's born with it, or maybe she got it from a box of hair dye. Either way, choosing to go red is a damn vivid choice. It means you want to join in on all of the things that make a redhead a red—like our reputation for being fiery, all of the eyes turning to you, and embracing a hair color that's truly magnificent. While some natural redheads have mixed feelings about dyed redheads, the truth is that to opt into red hair is to stand proudly with us and say, "Yes, this really is the best lifestyle."

So, if you're a dyed red, then let me just say this: welcome, and you've made the right choice. And to properly admit you into our redhead society, we have insider tips that should make your journey a whole lot smoother. After all, our hair color is exciting, daring, and most of all, fun—so we don't blame you for wanting to come to the red side!

Pick Your Red Poison

There's that song in *Pocahontas* where she sings, "Can you paint with all the colors of the wind?" and truly, just change the word "wind" to "red" and that's the challenge facing someone who's about to dye their hair red. Because there are so many shades, and trying to find the exact right one can feel a lot like trying to disarm a bomb (yes, it's exactly that intense, don't question me). So use the below as a guide to get you started, or restarted, on your journey into the ginger world.

If your skin is on the fairer side, go for light strawberry, copper, muted ginger, golden, or a more carroty auburn. "Carrot" isn't exactly the color you want to think about, but when that bright orange has a touch of auburn with it, it's just amazing for those more porcelain skin tones. And avoid burgundy or wine-inspired red dyes, as they'll likely wash your complexion out.

If you're a medium skin tone, you can try out a darker auburn, coppery blond, or golden red. And if you're too nervous to go full red, snagging some copper highlights will add just enough red to your hair to give it a good punch.

Have darker skin? Look for berry- or wine-colored reds if you want a pop of color. Or if you want something really bold, like Rihanna's red, choose a blue-red. If subtlety is more your thing, then a deep auburn or chestnut hue will keep the red light and more natural looking.

INSPIRATIONAL FAKE REDS

Molly Ringwald

JULIA ROBERTS

DAVID BOWIE

Christina Hendricks

Gillian Anderson

Benedict Cumberbatch

EDDIE REDMAYNE

AMY ADAMS

Emma Stone

Alyson Hannigan

Deborah Ann Woll

LAURA PREPON

CYNTHIA NIXON

Brittany Snow

Carey Mulligan

six

The Badass History of Reds

From Warriors to Poets, We've Come a Long Way

A famous animated redhead once said, "I'm not bad. I'm just drawn that way," which is actually pretty accurate for how we wound up with a lot of the stereotypes about redheads today. Because even though we're not all fiery sex bombs, comedians, or bullies, people take one look at us and assume that must be the case. They draw us into the boxes where they think we fit best. But why do people think they understand us even before they get to know us? In large part, how norms feel about us today is due to how they've viewed us historically. And to fully appreciate how far reds have come, we need to examine where we came from.

HISTORICAL MOMENTS WHEN RED HAIR WAS A *GOOD* THING

Many people assume that red hair first popped up in Ireland, or Scotland, or one of those Northern European places where populations of people with red hair are now the largest. (Scotland's currently in the lead with 13 percent of their population being ginge.) But in reality the gene for red hair appeared around fifty thousand years ago, when early humans were migrating from Africa and settling in Central Asia.[21] That migration and spread of the population is how Harvard researchers came to find Neanderthal remains in El Sidrón, Spain, and Monti Lessini, Italy. Those remains both held the *MC1R* gene. So in other words, the remains of a 43,000-year-old and 50,000-year-old Neanderthal were both found to have the gene for red hair.[22] And neither of them were discovered in Scotland. To be clear, Neanderthal's had all kinds of hair colors—but this discovery showed that red hair has been around since early man, and therefore isn't a more recent evolutionary change. It's also important to note that the tinge of ginge found in the DNA of those Neanderthals is not the same as the red hair we humans have today. The genetic *MC1R* mutation found in Neanderthals can't be found in modern humans today. We both carried that *MC1R* gene, but our respective reds are the result of two very different mutations on that gene.[23]

But you may be wondering: what does this have to do with me? It's important to know where we came from because so much of our early history as gingers took place in areas you might be surprised by. Like in Turkey, Bulgaria, and Greece, where a people known as the Thracians began to exist circa 1000 BC.[24] If that name sounds at all familiar, you might remember reading about them as being allies to the Trojans in the *Iliad* by Homer.[25] If you didn't read the *Iliad,* that's OK too. Because the important thing to us reds here is that the Thracians worshipped gods with red hair and blue eyes. And if you're wondering why they chose to worship reds (other than the obvious fact that we're demigods*), it's because the Thracians themselves had a large population of gingers, so they worshipped the gods they most resembled. Similarly, as Marion Roach discusses in her book *The Roots of Desire,* the Celts had some flame-haired gods, which was likely the result of their flame-haired population. For example, one of those ginger gods was named Morrigan, and she was a goddess of war and fertility. Hmm . . . war and fertility. Kind of like fiery reds and sultry reds, but all in one convenient goddess. Very interesting indeed!

And the color red, as we've discussed, can often be viewed as a power color, eliciting feelings of strength and anger. Which might explain why certain Egyptian rulers chose to rule with red henna in their hair. Like Ramses II, who ruled in the 1200s BC and is often acknowledged as one of the most influential and powerful pharaohs.[26] Similarly, Cleopatra, who ruled over Egypt for more than twenty years, chose to be on the throne with henna-red hair. (Don't worry, I'll be talking a great deal more about our pal Cleo later in the chapter.)

---

* Probably? Definitely.

Indeed, redheads have often found great success when seated on a throne. (Which begs the question: why aren't we all doing that right this moment?) And if you don't believe me, then look no further than the English monarchy. Because, damn it, they have had so many gingers in power (Prince Harry being the modern result of that). Let's start with King Henry II. He (and his tinge of ginge) ruled from 1154—1189, and while he was known for having a menacing temper, many scholars have credited him with laying the path to create a unified Britain. Right after Henry came his son, King Richard I, who earned his nickname "the Lion Heart" because he was an excellent strategist and fighter. Then there was Elizabeth Woodville, queen consort of England, who sat on the English throne from 1464 to 1483, and whose portraits often depict her with red hair. Immediately after Woodville came Elizabeth of York, who was the first Tudor queen consort in that family's history and sat on the throne alongside her husband, Henry VII, from 1486 until her death in 1503. The infamous King Henry VIII and his brother Arthur were both gingers, and Henry's first wife, Catherine of Aragon, had dark auburn hair. King Henry VIII, as you may remember from history books or binge watching *The Tudors*, had six wives and was a bit of a tyrant and egomaniac. He'd pass policies that were good for him (e.g., separating the Church of England from the Roman Catholic Church so that he could have his marriage annulled), and executed two of his wives. Nice guy, right? His first wife, Catherine, gave birth to the ginger Queen Mary I, who ruled from 1553 to 1558 but wasn't a very popular queen, mainly because of her propensity for persecuting Protestants. She became known as "Bloody Mary" for that one. But before Queen Mary I's reign, there was Lady Jane Grey, who's more popularly known as the Nine-Day Queen. That's because she was on the throne for a short nine days before being executed for treason by Queen Mary I. Lady

David Fisher/REX/Shutterstock.com

Jane Grey was also a ginger. After Mary's death, her half sister, Queen Elizabeth I, took the throne and ruled from 1558 to 1603. She's regarded as a successful and respected ruler, but I'll delve more into her accomplishments later. Let's also note that during the Elizabethan era red hair became pretty damn fashionable. And the nobility attempted to emulate their queen's look through wigs and dye. Talk about a royal impact. Meanwhile, over in Scotland, there was Alexander II, who had red hair and ruled from 1214 to 1249. He was known for working with England to define and recognize the territories of Scotland, officially making it a kingdom. Not too shabby, my red royals.

But the fun doesn't end there, because we haven't even gotten into how
we influenced not only the political world but the art world as well. When
you walk into a museum, you'll undeniably see what I'm talking about. From
Botticelli's *The Birth of Venus*, Gustav Klimt's *Danaë*, Degas's *Dancers*, and
Edvard Munch's *Lady from the Sea*, it's clear artists have always known how
to appreciate redheads (well, the ladies at least). And by "appreciate," I of
course mean that they understood how to showcase a redhead in some state of
undress.

Red-haired vixens even crept into religious paintings: Mary Magdalene, for
example, was often portrayed as a redhead. Just take a look at *Mary Magdalene
in a Grotto,* by Jules Joseph Lefebvre, or the *Repentant Mary Magdalene,* by
Giovanni Pedrini Giampietrino. These images of Mary not only show flowing
red hair, but she's often a little exposed . . . like, boobs, mainly. While there's
no evidence in the Bible that Mary was a prostitute, the popular belief is that
she was. And at the very least, Mary *was* a sinner. So even though Magdalene
was most certainly dark skinned with dark hair IRL, because she was believed
to be a sinner (a.k.a. a woman on the hunt for sex), she automatically got that
crimson touch in the art world.

by Sandro Botticelli

When you think about these moments and the people behind them, some of those stereotypes that exist about redheads start to make more sense. Like, the fact that we have these rulers in our past with bad tempers (looking at you, King Henry II), and we're often known as fiery in the present day. Or that we were continuously depicted in the art world as sinners who couldn't seem to keep our clothes on, and those pieces of art helped feed the stereotype that we're vixens today. For better or worse, our past, while most certainly in the past, has helped form our current situation.

HISTORICAL MOMENTS WHEN RED HAIR *WASN'T* AS GREAT

If going through puberty as a ginger teaches you anything, it's that people aren't terribly kind to reds these days. And, perhaps not surprisingly, there were plenty of examples of less-than-friendly behavior toward our hair color throughout history.

Since we discussed the fact that certain Egyptian rulers put henna in their hair so they could rule as reds, it's only fair to start this off by talking about just how complicated a relationship the Egyptians had with red hair. At various points red hair was worshipped. For example, we talked about the god Set, who was all about chaos and storms. Sometimes the Egyptians worshipped him, and at other times he was vilified. The people who worshipped Osiris (Set's brother) were a particularly nasty sort. See, they were more than a little ticked off that Set killed Osiris, so in order to honor their slain god they sacrificed redheads because, unfortunately for them, they had the hair color of Set.[29]

Things weren't much better over in ancient Greece, where redheads were viewed as barbarians. As Jacky Colliss Harvey details in her book *Red: A History of the Redhead*, this was due in large part to the Thracians. Remember them from earlier? The people who worshipped ginger gods because so many of them were gingers? OK, well on top of that, the Thracians also had customs that, to the Greeks, made them equivalent to your hillbilly uncle. Things like practicing polygamy and selling unwanted children into slavery top the list of Thracian no good, very bad things. So right off the bat: the Greeks just thought the flame-haired Thracians were savages.

And this is about to get weird and uncomfortable so grab your anxiety pet if you need it. Because the Thracian children that were sold into slavery were often bought by Athenian households, and, as you may have guessed, the children were occasionally redheads. This was such a prevalent practice and occurrence that slaves were actually depicted with red hair on the Greek stage as well.[30] It was around the second century AD that the first Greek thesaurus, called the *Onomasticon*, was written. In that work, the author lists the seven different kinds of slaves depicted in Greek theater. You read that correctly: because so many relationships in ancient Greece revolved around a master's relationship with his slaves, those relationships were often depicted onstage as well. And of the seven types of slaves that writers would depict, four of those were described as having red hair. Thus, performers in Greek and Roman theater were given red wigs to identify them as slaves. If you were a slave in ancient Greece, you were viewed as less than and a bit dimwitted (remember, the Greeks had very specific ideas about who the Thracians were). As a result, those redheaded slaves would often serve as clumsy comic relief onstage. Which likely also has contributed to our view of reds as comic relief in the present day.

Did You Know . . . ?

Ancient Hindu priests would try to cure jaundice by applying the hairs of a red bull to a patient's skin.[31]

We've also touched on the connection between red hair and a perceived Jewishness. As we discussed, many Jews had and still have red hair. And because ginger locks are such a strong identifying marker, evil figures in culture were often depicted with red hair to show that this person was Jewish. Just look at artistic renderings of Judas and how often he's got a tinge of ginge, if you don't believe me. Authors Jacky Colliss Harvey and Marion Roach both did extensive research into the connections between anti-Semitism and red hair, noting that the link is easily seen in Shakespeare's plays. Keep in mind that during Shakespeare's time, his plays were performed to audiences who'd likely never seen a Jewish person in real life. In England, the Jews had been expelled in 1290, and they weren't readmitted until 1656. So when we look at a play like *The Merchant of Venice*, which premiered in the 1590s, and see that Shakespeare had the Jewish moneylender character of Shylock wear a red wig, it's not a stretch to assume that Shakespeare used that wig color to signal to the audience that this character was Jewish. And for those who need a refresher, Shylock is a manipulative moneylender who's hell-bent on revenge (evil redhead, much?). Not to mention a line in *Macbeth*, added sometime after 1616 in a revision by playwright Thomas Middleton, where a magic spell calls for "three ounces of the red-haired wench." And, as Harvey points out, scholars believe this hair-color reference is meant to be seen as an allusion to lechery and Jewishness. Basically, if you were a red-haired man in Europe, people assumed a lot about you just based on your looks. But if you were a Jewish redhead, those assumptions became exponentially worse.

And to top that off, there were some pretty nutty historical assumptions about gingers. One being the Romanian belief (circa the 1800s) that if you had red hair, you'd come back as a vampire after death.[32] And another being that if you had sex while a woman was menstruating, your offspring would be marked with red hair. After all, we're dealing with a recessive gene, which means parents who lack red hair can end up with a red-haired child. Which must have been pretty damn confusing for people having babies before science came around to explain things. But there were plenty of myths to clarify that occurrence—one being that red hair was a sign your child had been chosen by the devil.[33] These beliefs existed in many cultures and were the result of plain ignorance.

Much of how we were treated historically has influenced how we're perceived today. Norms still can't shake the feeling that we're evil—that's clear in our pop culture depictions. And whether it's because people are frightened by our otherness or they secretly think we're all barbarians, we've become the targets of physical attacks through Kick a Ginger Day. Is it unfair? Hell yes, but what doesn't kill us makes us redder and better. Plus, nothing can kill us because we're vamp . . . I mean, indestructible forces of pure greatness.

INSPIRATIONAL *REDS THROUGHOUT HISTORY*

If you thumb through the glossary of historical redheads, you'll start to see a pattern emerge: we veer toward the zero-fucks-given end of the spectrum. We reds are renegades, fearless fighters, and innovative artists. We've led armies into battle, discovered treatments for diseases, and left enormous impressions on the art world. Which means the rumors are true: centuries ago, one of our redhead brethren cast a spell from the blood of youths to fill us all with unlimited potential. OK, there was no ancient witch. But with so many redhead icons floating around, it does make you wonder: how did all of these incredible historical figures also just happen to be gingers? In that spirit, let's look at the historical reds who've made our hair color proud—the poets, the activists, and the athletes—and we can decide for ourselves whether that ginger color gave them a strand up in the world.

JAMES DEAN-ESQUE REBELS   RED-HEADS   BOSSES WHO GOT SHIT DONE

WHICH LEADER WOULD YOU RATHER BE:
Boudicca or Queen Elizabeth I?

Boudicca: The Brits love a good redhead, and that all started with Boudicca: she was the first recorded redhead British queen, and the ultimate badass. Her husband, Prasutagus, died in AD 60. He was the ruler of the Iceni people of eastern Britain, but with his death, the Romans (who had conquered much of Britain) decided they would annex and plunder his kingdom and take his lands. Essentially, Boudicca and her people were fucked. Boudicca was just thirty years old when the Romans tried to crush her family by flogging her

and raping her daughters. Really sweet folks, right? Boudicca wasn't about to let that stop her, though. In retaliation, she decided to fight back against the Roman invaders. The Iceni people rallied around her as she called for revenge. She burned what is now known as London to the ground with an estimated hundred thousand warriors by her side.[34] Images of her now show a fierce woman with flowing red hair, riding a chariot into battle. Queen Boudicca eventually lost the fight. But rather than let the Romans kill her and her family, she poisoned herself and her daughters to avoid being captured. Reds, ya know, we're something else.

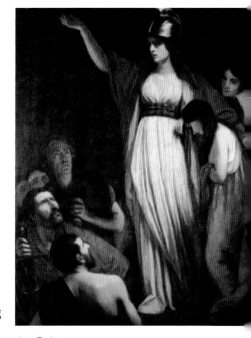

Jon Opie

Queen Elizabeth I: When you hear the word "queen" do you think of jewels and beautiful clothing? Because Queen Elizabeth I definitely embodied that picture of royalty in her later years, along with being thoughtful, intelligent, and a damn revolutionary. The arts flourished under her reign, as did voyages of discovery. And, being the spitfire she was, Queen Elizabeth I was known to ride through the country on horseback rather than in a carriage, which was the custom for noblewomen at the time. She came to power when she was just twenty-five years old in 1558 and inherited a country in bankruptcy that faced threats of invasion from numerous countries. Not a great spot to be in! She eventually had to take on a war with Spain, which she guided England in winning. Queen Elizabeth I never married, and by all accounts had no interest in sharing her power with a man. Clever girl. She spent close to forty-five years on the throne, bringing stability to the country and leaving a legacy of progress in her wake. How's that for a job well done?

The "Darnley Portrait"

WHICH SCIENTIST WOULD YOU RATHER BE:
Galileo Galilei or Gertrude Elion?

Galileo Galilei: Trailblazers are pretty great, and that's exactly what Galileo was in the early 1600s. He published papers shooting down Aristotle's theory that everything revolved around the earth and openly supported Copernicus's theories that everything revolved around the sun. His theories ended up landing Galileo under house arrest in 1633 (where he remained until he died in 1642), because at the time, what he was saying was considered blasphemy against the Catholic Church.

But while the church took away Galileo's freedom, it couldn't take away his scientific achievements. He invented a telescope that allowed him to look at the moon and see that it was not a perfect sphere—as scientists previously believed—but round and dotted with mountains and craters (similar to Earth). He also used his telescope to discover four of the moons orbiting Jupiter and made other key observations about the Milky Way, Venus, and sunspots. His legacy is that he's widely known as the father of modern physics. Not a bad red to model your life after.

Gertrude Elion: Would you rather be a Nobel Prize winner? Then look no further than Gertrude Elion, who won the Nobel for medicine in 1988. She was a biochemist and pharmacologist who helped create a number of medications to treat a variety of diseases, including drugs to treat leukemia, malaria, herpes, cancer, and AIDS. Her innovative research would eventually lead to the important development of the drug AZT, which helps prevent and treat HIV/AIDS. In addition to changing people's actual day-to-day lives, she holds forty-five patents, twenty-three honorary degrees, and was the first woman inducted into the National Inventors Hall of Fame. She died in 1999 at the age of eighty-one. Also, she said this awesome thing: "Don't be afraid of hard work. Nothing worthwhile comes easily. Don't let others discourage you or tell you that you can't do it. In my day I was told women didn't go into chemistry. I saw no reason why we couldn't."

WHICH ARTIST WOULD YOU RATHER BE:
Vincent van Gogh or Elizabeth Siddal?

Vincent van Gogh: Does this name sound familiar? If it doesn't, then you need to find a time machine and redo your life. Van Gogh was born in 1853 in the Netherlands and lived in poverty. He only sold one painting while he was alive and relied on his brother, Theo, for money. Only after his death in 1890, when he killed himself at the age of thirty-seven, did his work really become appreciated. He's been cited as one of the major influences behind the abstract expressionism of the 1940s and 1950s. He was a misunderstood genius who left an impact. And it's not hard to see how his vibrant use of colors and unique painting techniques influenced countless other painters. Just look at *Vase with Fifteen Sunflowers, The Red Vineyard,* or *Poppies,* and you'll undoubtedly understand his lasting fame.

Heidi Blomster/Heblo/Pixaby

"Beata Beatrix," Dante Gabriel Rossetti, via Wikimedia Commons

Elizabeth Siddal: Oh, to be an artist's muse in the 1800s: such was the life of Elizabeth Siddal. At twenty years old, she was discovered by the artist Walter Deverell. He painted her as Viola in his piece *Twelfth Night*, based on Shakespeare's play—it was the first painting she ever sat for. Siddal was then introduced to the Pre-Raphaelite brotherhood, a group of English painters, poets, and critics, who would go on to use her as their muse in several works. Aside from Walter Deverell, she modeled for William Holman Hunt, John Everett Millais, and, most prominently, for Dante Gabriel Rossetti. It was Rossetti who truly obsessed over her likeness, using her to model for such famous paintings as *Beata Beatrix, Dante's Vision of Rachel and Leah*, and *Regina Cordium*. Her flowing red hair is prominent in all of them, naturally. Siddal eventually became Rossetti's lover, and the two had an on-again, off-again relationship for several years before they were married. But the stress from her relationship with Rossetti led to bouts of depression, which were then treated with laudanum, which she became addicted to. She and Rossetti married in 1860, and while she was still suffering from addiction, she became pregnant in 1861 and gave birth to a stillborn daughter. It's believed that she had postpartum depression after this event, which may have led to her eventual overdose on laudanum in 1862. She was also just thirty-two years old.

Siddal wasn't just a muse. During her life she was also an artist in her own right. Her love of reading poetry led to a love of writing poetry, and being surrounded by painters allowed her to study with them. Soon Siddal began to draw, sketch, and paint her own pieces. So while her likeness lives on through the famous artists she posed for, her own art has a lasting place in the world as well.

WHICH ATHLETE WOULD YOU RATHER BE:
Shaun White or Red Grange?

Shaun White: "The Flying Tomato" is one hell of a new ginger nickname if I've ever heard one, but that moniker just so happens to belong to all-around mega-athlete Shaun White. White began snowboarding at the age of six and earned sponsorship by the age of seven. Let's take a moment to think about where we all were at seven years old, and then remember where White was. Yeah, big achievement. So back to snowboarding: White's participated in three winter Olympics games so far and taken home two gold medals in the half-pipe. And from 2002 to 2013 he competed in the winter X Games, where he earned thirteen gold medals, three silver, and two bronze. But the athletic fun doesn't stop there, because White went pro as a skateboarder at the age of seventeen. He's racked up quite a lot of awards in general, but for skateboarding he's the proud winner of two gold medals, two silver, and one bronze in X Games competitions.

And if all that's not enough to leave you thinking, *What am I doing with my life?* then just wait, because White's expanded his career *again* to include playing in a band called Bad Things and overseeing Shaun White Enterprises as the chief executive, managing a clothing line and sponsorship deals. Dude is a ginger overachiever.

Red Grange: "Red" is no "Flying Tomato" when it comes to nicknames, but Red Grange's hair was just as iconic. He's one of the most important and successful football players of all time, so when it comes to legends in the sports world, it's hard to top this guy. Red was born in 1903 and began playing football in high school. But in college Red really shined: he scored at least one touchdown in every game he played except for one and was on the cover of *Time* as a college senior. There's a statue erected in his honor at the University of Illinois, where he played college ball, and he was named the number 1 player in college football history by ESPN and one of the greatest football players of all time by *The Sporting News*. Not a bad way to leave your alma mater.

After college, Red signed a contract with the Chicago Bears in 1925 that was unprecedented—Red was guaranteed at least $3,000 per game, plus a cut of the gate receipts, according to ESPN. To put that in perspective, most players could expect about $100 a game, so Red made bank. That's because football wasn't exactly the glorified sport it is today, and Red earned the big paycheck because his performances brought out enormous crowds. In fact, the crowds were so massive that he's credited with legitimizing the NFL. (That movie *Leatherheads* starring George Clooney is loosely based on Red.)

Red retired from football in 1934 after leading the Bears to several championship games and performing game-changing moves that are still remembered to this day. He also had a career off the field, starring in silent films like *One Minute to Play* and working as a sports announcer for CBS and NBC.

WHICH POET WOULD YOU RATHER BE:
Emily Dickinson or William Blake?

Emily Dickinson: Much like Van Gogh, it was only after death that Emily Dickinson achieved any real acclaim—something that Emily might be horrified by, considering how intensely private she was. But whether she's rolling over in her grave or not, she's now considered one of the most significant American poets of all time. She wrote nearly 1,800 poems, only a select few of which were published before her death. And if you're looking to brush up on your poetry knowledge, check out her pieces "Success is counted sweetest," "Because I could not stop for Death," and "I taste a liquor never brewed." Emily lived at home with her parents and in later years rarely left the safety of her own bedroom. The Dickinson family was prominent, but Emily was considered an eccentric in her community. And her poetry reflected her unconventional lifestyle—it often lacked titles, used capitalization irregularly, and had an overall original style. Her lines were innovative, covering topics from joy to death to religion, and helped earn her a place among the most influential artists in America. She died at the age of fifty-five in her bedroom, which, let's be honest, is probably just as she would've wanted it.

William Blake: If you've ever seen or read the *Red Dragon* installment of the Hannibal franchise, then you may already be familiar with some of Blake's work. His painting *The Great Red Dragon and the Woman Clothed in Sun* played a prominent role in the storyline of the book, TV, and film adaptations. But for those who aren't familiar, let me introduce you to one of the seminal figures of the Romantic age: William Blake, primarily known for his work in poetry and the visual arts.

"Portrait of William Blake," by Thomas Phillips

Blake's childhood was spent in London in the 1700s, and by all accounts he was unusual. For example, he claimed to have visions, which he continued to see into adulthood. At the age of twenty-six, he published his first book of poetry, called *Poetical Sketches.* Next came his most well received poetry collection, *Songs of Innocence,* in 1789, followed by *Songs of Experience* in 1794. In his lifetime, Blake was not well known for either his poetry or paintings. Poor lad. He published works and displayed his art at shows but wasn't truly recognized for them. It was only after death that his fame in the literary and art world really came to be. (Why does it always have to be *after* death?!) And his influence on the modernist movement and on poets like W. B. Yeats, as well as beat poets like Allen Ginsberg, has ensured that his legacy carries on. Plus, all those Hannibal movies and TV shows don't hurt.

WHICH WRITER WOULD YOU RATHER BE: *James Joyce or Bram Stoker?*

James Joyce: Would you want to be one of the most influential writers of the twentieth century? Let's talk a bit about Joyce before you decide. He was a modernist writer and his work was both complex and controversial. For example, *Ulysses*, which is often regarded as one of the greatest novels ever written, prompted a censorship battle

Flickr/Creative Commons/poppet with a camera

in the publishing world, because some thought the content was obscene and pornographic. (Thankfully, Joyce and his publishers won that battle.) Joyce was the oldest of ten children and was exceptionally smart. As a young writer, he was rejected many times over, until the publication of his short-story collection, *Dubliners*, in 1914. After that, he published *A Portrait of the Artist as a Young Man* in 1916, *Ulysses* in 1922, and *Finnegans Wake* in 1939. He was on literary fire, so to speak. While Joyce didn't need to wait until after death for fame, he did have problems in his life: he was lousy with money and spent it all on luxurious hotels and furs for his wife and daughter. He also suffered from atrocious eyesight, and at times was essentially blind. He passed away at the age of fifty-eight from peritonitis brought on by a perforated ulcer, but he left quite a literary legacy in his wake.

Bram Stoker: Want to know who to thank for all those vampire TV shows? While Bram Stoker wrote many novels (twelve fiction books in total), it's *Dracula* that he's most well known for. He was called a "red-haired giant" by his biographer, and indeed he was a bit of a lumberjack of a ginger. Stoker published *Dracula* in 1897, and it was an instant success. But even before that, he had lived a life surrounded by artists and creatives—he met Henry Irving, a famous actor, when he was twenty-nine years old and began a lifelong friendship and business relationship with him. He was the manager of Irving's theater for twenty-seven years  and came into contact with figures like Mark Twain (a fellow redhead), Oscar Wilde, and Theodore Roosevelt, among others. Stoker was known as extremely energetic and versatile when it came to his talents—he wrote as a theater critic for a local newspaper, founded the Dublin Sketching Club for artists, and traveled extensively. He married a woman named Florence Balcombe, who at one point was being pursued by Oscar Wilde but opted to marry Stoker instead. He died at the age of sixty-four after a number of strokes, but his vampire legacy lives on. (A red writing a vampire story? Add that to the "gingers are vampires" fire.)

WHICH ACTIVIST WOULD YOU RATHER BE:
Lucy Burns or Barbara Castle?

Lucy Burns: How would you like to be credited with being one of the most important figures in women's rights history? Such is the legacy of Lucy Burns, whose flame-red hair undoubtedly inspired her to do enormous things for us ladies. Burns was born in 1879, a time not terribly exceptional for women, but her father pushed for female education, and as a result, Burns was highly educated—she was one of the first women to attend Yale University's graduate school. While spending a summer at Oxford in England, she was introduced to the Women's Social and Political Union (WSPU), which was dedicated to fighting for women's rights in the United Kingdom.

When she eventually returned to the United States, she helped form the National Woman's Party, whose primary goal was to give women the right to vote. And Burns was incredibly instrumental within that party as the chief organizer, suffrage educator, and media correspondent, among other duties. She was jailed numerous times for her protests and spent more time in jail than any other suffragist of that time. One jail stint in particular was dubbed the "Night of Terror" after Burns and other female protestors were brutally beaten and not given medical attention. On that night, Burns's hands were handcuffed above her head; she was so well respected that her cellmates held their hands above their heads in solidarity. In other words: Burns was nothing less than a fighter. Burns and the NWP were effective in pressuring the United States government to pass the Nineteenth Amendment giving women the right to vote. As soon as she'd accomplished that, Burns retired from the movement and dedicated herself to helping raise her orphaned niece. And that niece certainly had quite a role model to look up to.

Barbara Castle: How would you like to be a prolific politician in the British government? Sure, the queen gets to live in that big castle, but after you learn more about Barbara, you'll probably rather be her. She's been credited as the most important female politician the Labour Party has ever had, and she held an office of some sort for over thirty years. Her nickname was the "Red Queen," and she was known for being incredibly hardworking, forceful in achieving her goals, and unwilling to back down. When she served as the minister of transport (1965–68), she did two very important things: passed legislation requiring that all new cars be outfitted with seat belts and brought Breathalyzers into the mainstream in the United Kingdom to combat that pesky problem of drunk drivers. Thank you, Barbara Castle!

Then when she served as Secretary of State for Employment (1968–70), she helped her fellow ladies out by putting through the Equal Pay Act of 1970, which demanded that women be paid as much as their male counterparts. The 2010 movie *Made in Dagenham* is all about how Castle reacted when a group of women went on strike at a factory, and the role she played in getting the Equal Pay Act passed. She was a feminist who refused to see the working women around her treated less fairly than men. Pretty boss move, if you ask me. Not to mention that she also worked on things like welfare reform, pensions for disabled people, and an allowance for single women who gave up their jobs to take care of invalid or disabled members of their family. Let's give a standing ovation to Castle!

WHICH FAKE REDHEAD WOULD YOU RATHER BE: Cleopatra or Lucille Ball?

Cleopatra: In the ginger world there's a long-held belief that Cleopatra was, in fact, a red. This theory isn't rooted in pure fantasy, because as Egyptologist Joann Fletcher details in her book *Cleopatra the Great*, a fresco unearthed in Pompeii is believed to depict Cleopatra, and it portrays a woman with bright red hair. The truth about the Egyptians, though, is that they were real lovers of wigs and hair dye. And since Cleopatra's ancestry was Greek (though she was born in Egypt), the likelihood of her naturally having red hair isn't high. Keep praying to Amun-Ra for that one.

Flickr/Creative Commons/Kyle Rush

Whether Cleopatra dyed her hair red or simply wore a red wig, she was clearly a lover of the color, and for that we have to welcome her with open arms. And even if you don't know much about Cleopatra, you certainly know her name. That's because she's an honorary red who left a lasting impression. She ruled over Egypt for almost three decades as a coregent, sharing power with her two younger brothers and eventually her son. But it was always Cleopatra who took the lead regardless of who sat beside her. She was also incredibly well educated, reportedly speaking a dozen languages and mastering math, science, and philosophy. And while pop culture has made her looks the main focus of her success, it was truly her charm and wit that helped her gain allies and succeed as a ruler. She was the last active pharaoh of Egypt, and red hair was part of that legacy.

Lucille Ball: OK, so there's the appeal of an honorary red who ruled over Egypt, but what about one of the most iconic comedians of all time? If you're one of those who had no idea Lucy wasn't a natural ginger, then I'm sorry to be the bearer of this news. However, she dyed her hair and found more success because of it, so she's an honorary red for that.

GTV Archive/REX/
Shutterstock.com

While Lucy started off her career with roles in B movies, she eventually got noticed after doing a radio program where she played a housewife. CBS wanted her to develop it for the small screen. But as a woman who knew what she wanted, she agreed to play the role only if her real-life husband could costar with her. When the network refused, she and Desi Arnaz created a traveling vaudeville show similar to *I Love Lucy*. With the success of that act, the network gave Lucy what she wanted, and *I Love Lucy* made its debut in 1951. The show ran for six seasons and was number one in the country for four of those seasons. Pretty impressive stuff.

Lucy was the first female business head of a TV-production company when she served as vice president of Desilu Productions, which produced not only *I Love Lucy*, but also such iconic shows as *The Untouchables, Mission: Impossible, The Lucy Show*, and *Star Trek*. And she later went on to found her own production company called Lucille Ball Productions. It's not hard to see that Lucy wasn't just a funny red but a badass boss red as well. Lucy died at the age of seventy-seven, but her legacy continues to live on and has inspired many other comedians. There's even an annual Lucille Ball Comedy Festival held in New York that celebrates new comedians, as well as Lucy's achievements. She is one helluva honorary red.

Here's What Happens When You Really Love Lucy

In case you're wondering what I wanted to be when I grew up, the answer is Lucy Ricardo in *I Love Lucy*. Didn't matter that it wasn't a real job, that was going to be my reality. I would live in New York, have my best friend (Elisa) in the same building, and be married to a very talented and handsome Cuban man. And at the end of a long day, I'd put on my silk robe, Ricky and I would kiss each other goodnight, and then we'd climb into separate beds. My future was BRIGHT. But in the spirit of honesty, the man and building BFF weren't really why I wanted to be Lucy. I wanted to make people laugh. I wanted to try dumb shit and have even dumber shit happen. I'd be the person who could turn the most mundane activity, like shopping for hats, into a harrowing (but hilarious) experience.

I watched reruns of *I Love Lucy* right before bed and started to glean that trying new things and saying whatever was on my mind would likely translate into laughs. I decided it was a good idea to lock our math teacher out of the classroom in the fourth grade, for example. Sure enough, everyone laughed. I got a detention, but it all seemed worth it. And when my friends dared me to steal an entire tray of cookies from the second-graders' field day, I did it. Again, lots of laughs and lots of detention slips. In my history class, when Mrs. Brown told me to stop chewing gum, I popped another stick in my mouth, raised my eyebrows, and said, "Why, want a piece?" We didn't have superlatives in middle school, but if we had I definitely would've gotten Most Likely to Be an Ass to Teachers.

Women aren't always encouraged to be the funniest or loudest people in the room. We're told to be ladylike and behave. And, honestly, who even knows what that means? Sit in an antique chair, balance a teacup in a saucer, and never EVER allow a fart to leave your body? All I knew was that Lucy wasn't ladylike, and she didn't give a fuck about whatever the norms were up to. Watching her encouraged me to amp up my sassiness and keep getting into trouble, because if I did, then I'd get big laughs, just like Lucy. I'd contort my face into the most hideous expression and turn to my mom and say, "This is my impression of you." Which sounds mean but always made her laugh. I'd dress my brother and me in my parents' clothes, and we'd parade around the house until my dad noticed and smiled. I joined a theater troop in middle school and always volunteered for the role of "girl who heaves her body around the stage and speaks in a heinous accent." I loved shocking people and pushing boundaries, something that Lucy Ricardo, our honorary ginger, taught me to do. So while I didn't grow up to exactly be Lucy, I like to think she has something to do with all those hours I spent in detention.

seven

Raising a Little Red

It's Not Easy Being a Lotto Winner

Maybe you've already got a little red you're in the midst of raising. Maybe you're knocked up. Or perhaps you're single and the closest thing to a relationship is the one you have with cheese. Either way, there's no denying the power of a ginger baby. Even if you hate kids and never want 'em, if you say you don't think redhead babies are cute, you're just lying. To see a baseball-size head (Is that how large baby heads are? Whatever, they're *small!*) covered in bright red hair will illicit the same kind of "squeeee!" sound you make whenever you see a cute dog with its tongue sticking out: it's just adorable, plain and simple.

Unfortunately, not everyone gets to be **#blessed** with a ginger baby, and the odds of having one are slim. So if you are one of the lucky few, then it's time to have some real talk: because having a red baby will be different, especially if you're a norm. Baby reds come with special rules, and this chapter will make sure you know them all so you can raise that red to take over the world someday, or whatever else they want to do. And if you grew up as a red, think of this as a refresher in what it's like to be a ginger kid. Either way, you're going to know all the insider secrets to raising the most amazing child with the very best head of hair.

THE BIG RED CONNECTION

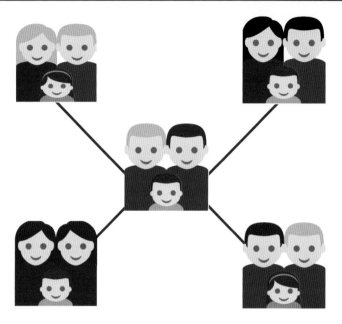

Do you have a baby red? Well, congratulations, because that means you've won the lottery! To get a redhead baby, you need so many things to go right. We're the Goldilocks (so to speak) of the hair world. The genes and timing have to be *just* right in order to even stand a chance of producing one of us. At the very minimum, both parents have to be carriers of the mutated *MC1R* redhead gene. And by "carrier," I mean that red hair is recessive, so even if you aren't a red, you could be carrying that gene. Here's how the math of making a baby red works: if one of the parents is a redhead and the other isn't but carries the redhead gene,

WHAT MAKES A REDHEAD MATH

| ONE REDHEAD PARENT | + | ANOTHER REDHEAD PARENT | = | 100 % CHANCE OF REDHEAD OFFSPRING |

ONE REDHEAD PARENT + *MC1R* CARRIER = 50 % CHANCE OF REDHEAD OFFSPRING

ONE *MC1R* CARRIER + ANOTHER *MC1R* CARRIER = 25 % CHANCE OF REDHEAD OFFSPRING

ONE *MC1R* CARRIER + A NON CARRIER = 0 % CHANCE OF REDHEAD OFFSPRING

there's a fifty-fifty chance you'll get a redhead child. If both parents are carriers but don't have red hair, you've got one in four odds, or a 25 percent shot. If both parents are ginger, you're looking at redhead city. But sadly, if even one parent doesn't hold that lucky *MC1R* gene, there's just no chance of seeing red.

Essentially, getting a baby red is a challenge, to say the least. The only sure way to get one is if you and your partner are both redheads. And if you're a norm, but carry the gene, then marrying a natural ginge increases your odds. But norms, if it makes you feel better, neither of my parents are actually redheads. My dad is a dark-haired Italian, and my mom is beautiful, blond, and Irish. Neither of them has red on their head. Which proves that two norms who carry that gene do have a chance.

For years I'd been told that red hair "skips a generation" and that I'd gotten it from my grandmother. But, thanks to science, I now know that I got my ginger locks from both sides of the family—my mom and dad's recessive *MC1R* genes. My parents had a 25 percent chance of getting me, and they nailed it. They then nailed it again when my little brother, also a redhead, was born. What can I say? Everything was *just* right.

BEING A PARENT *VS.* BEING A PARENT OF A RED

As the parent of a redhead, there will be a few awkward moments and some things that are wildly out of your control, but in the end you still get to live your life as a parent of a unicorn. And there's not much that can top that. So let's go ahead and compare what it's like to be a parent of a norm versus what it's like to be a parent of a baby red.

 Parent of a Norm: Strangers politely smile and coo at your baby.

 Parent of a Red: Strangers gawk, stare, and approach your child with the intent of engaging you both in conversation. They may even try to actually grab your child's hair, which is really weird.

Parent of a Norm: To meet like-minded parents, you go to a park, call a friend, or take a mommy-and-me class.

 Parent of a Red: To meet like-minded parents, you go online to search for other moms and dads with little reds. The truth is that as a parent of a red, chances are you won't meet many more like you. And you do need parents who can relate to what you're experiencing beyond the normal baby things—like, what's the best way to make your kid's hair really shine, and how do you handle it when a well-meaning friend asks if you're worried about your kid being bullied. That's when you'll want to talk to someone who's experienced the same thing, and that's where you may have to go online to find other parents of reds.

 Parent of a Norm: Teaches child how to say "hi" to new people so they're less shy.

 Parent of a Red: Teaches child to show some restraint, just a little, because they are definitely not shy. That whole not-at-all-shy thing happens because your child will inadvertently be made the center of attention when they're younger. They'll be used to people approaching them and to other kids staring (adults too), so they won't be living in a world where they're not admired. If anything, you might have to rein them in so they can give the other kids a fighting chance.

Parent of a Norm: A trip to the store takes an hour.

 Parent of a Red: A trip to the store takes an hour, plus an added thirty minutes. You and your kid will be stopped. People will feel compelled to tell you about their aunt who had red hair and the best sense of humor, and how your child's hair reminds them of those memories. Or how they themselves had a tint of red, and what a beautiful color it must be to stare at all day. You become a therapist, friend, and excellent listener as a parent of a red.

> My whole life, people have stared at me. I've just been so used to it, being a redhead, I think most redheads can relate to that.
>
> ALICIA WITT,
> NASHVILLE, JUSTIFIED, THE WALKING DEAD

 Parent of a Norm: Your kid has a temper tantrum.

Parent of a Red: Your kid has a temper tantrum *because* of their hair. Or at least that's what people will say. Anytime your child cries or gets fussy, which is a totally normal kid thing to do, whoever is there will blame it on that red hair color, "She's got that fiery temper!"

Parent of a Norm: You'll teach your child about loving their inner and outer beauty.

 Parent of a Red: You'll teach your child that they are not solely defined by their outer beauty and that there's more to them than this whole red-hair thing. Because their hair will be the first thing people notice, which may make them feel as if it's the most important thing. Of course, it's one BIG thing, but it's just the icing on the cake that is the person they are inside. So your conversations will have to rely more heavily on building up their confidence in their intelligence, charm, humor, and unique personality. Then, they'll be redheads on top of being extraordinary humans.

 Parent of a Norm: Your child gets bullied.

 Parent of a Red: Your child gets bullied about their hair color, something that they didn't choose to be born with. Luckily, being bullied is something you can easily talk to your children about. Because telling them to simply "get over it" isn't a great option. And when you do talk about their hair, use famous reds to emphasize that we do great things—look to Chapter Six for ideas on that. Because while so many others look the same, they get to stand out. It really does get better as you get older, and their hair will be a valuable asset they'll come to love (eventually).

Parent of a Norm: You're a parent!

 Parent of a Red: You're a parent who also happens to be part of the VIP (Very Important Parent) club. It's similar to that whole Gingers Unite-sighting thing—where redheads secretly acknowledge each other. Except that when you have a little ginge of your own, you'll get head nods and knowing glances from redheads and fellow parents of reds. You'll gain a whole new world of camaraderie without having to do any actual work. Ya know, except for the work of raising a tiny human. People who know what it's like to be red, or have a red, will quietly acknowledge that you're doing incredible work to keep our kind going.

THE PERKS OF A BABY GINGE

You've got this really cool item—a ginger kid—and when you hold it it's basically the same as having a Willy Wonka golden ticket. All you want to know is what this special and rare thing gets you. Is it the chance to own a candy factory?! Unlimited kittens for life?! Or a private island with a gourmet chef?! Well, not exactly, but there are definite advantages to having a child with a supernova on its head. I'll let you in on the most exquisite parts of the VIP club—you know, the things you can brag to your norm friends about.

PROS		CONS
LIKE A TINY CELEBRITY		ACTUALLY NOTHING
NEVER LOSE THEM IN A CROWD		
INARGUABLY CUTER		
HAIR THE COLOR OF SHERBET		

You'll never ever lose sight of them.

 This perk may seem a little obvious, but it's way more useful than you think and starts immediately when the baby is born. When you look into the crowded nursery, searching for your baby's face among many little faces, you'll be able to spot yours instantly by the ginger locks. Statistically speaking, your baby is likely to be the only one with a ginger mane, so you'll always be able to find them. This becomes even handier when your baby learns how to walk on its own, especially in public places. I speak from experience, since my brother and I were both gingers, and whenever my mom took us to the mall, we'd tend to run off in opposite directions, the way that a lot of kids do. However, it didn't take my mom long to find us darting between clothing racks. After all, how can you miss those bobs?

Not to mention, it just makes life simpler in terms of the "Where's my kid?" game. Class photos, sports teams, and field trips have the same perk. "Mine is the little redhead," is an easy way to tell someone which kid is yours.

You'll have a more naturally empathetic kid.

In an ideal lollipop-land of a world, reds wouldn't be bullied for their hair, period. But as it is, we go through life feeling like we're not part of the bigger group and are often the target of bullying. But the unexpected perk of this outsider-looking-in mentality is that we end up being significantly more accepting of differences and other people's individual qualities. Because if you're a kid who's bullied, you're compassionate toward other kids who might get bullied. Which, on average, tend to be the kids who are a little different from everyone else.

And in that same vein, the older your red gets, the more they'll come to understand that their hair is different, which is why they were singled out in the first place. But instead of resenting their hair, they'll start to appreciate how much it makes them stand out. And by fully comprehending their own rare beauty, they'll be better able to see the small but significant qualities that make everyone around them special. So instead of having a child who's prone to excluding others, you'll have one who embraces that otherness.

You're basically raising a little celebrity.

You may not think you'd ever have to utter, "Hi, my kid's eyes are *down there*," but believe me when I say that anyone who encounters your mini-you will want to fixate on their hair. It's like you have a tiny celebrity by your side at all times, and people just want to bask in their glow. They'll want to know where that hair came from, if they can touch it, and (especially if you're a norm) if the baby is even yours. I know, it sounds weird that someone would ask, "Is it yours?" But, to be fair to the norms, redheads look as if they were dropped from a rainbow and onto this earth solely for our viewing pleasure. Red hair can have a mystical quality, so you can't get too mad when someone understandably wonders if it's possible that this gorgeous thing is even human. Regardless though, your child will instantly be a topic of conversation, and one that you'll be well versed in discussing.

Cartoons become infinitely more fun.

As we discussed in the pop culture chapter, you can't turn on an animated anything without being bombarded by us. We're showing up as the protagonists, antagonists, sidekicks, and background characters in all of your kid's favorite movies and shows. And as a parent of a little red, it will be your job to "spot the ginge." It'll help them feel like they're represented on-screen and will just be a fun game for you when you're watching *Frozen* for the seventy-sixth time.

Other people will be jealous of your little red.

Ever watched one of those documentaries about people who win the lottery? It's all fun and money baths until other people who used to be their friends try to take the cash. Well hey, lotto winner, you've got a genetic prize that makes up just 2 percent of the world's population, which is going to make everyone else around you a little bit envious. After all, your kid is special, and not just because you say so.

EMPOWERING COSTUMES FOR LITTLE **REDS**

- Merida from *Brave*
- David Bowie
- Mystique from X-Men
- Ron Weasley from *Harry Potter*
- Ginger Spice (Girl Power!)
- Sally Skellington from *The Nightmare Before Christmas*

Your little ginge will have a leg up when it comes to health benefits.

 Let's all sing, "We're the best, arounddd . . ." Because, as we noted in the health chapter, there are definite benefits to being red. Like our ability to make vitamin D better than everyone else. And since we exist in a world where kids prefer being on their phone to being outside, that means you've got a kid who, even if they spend less time outdoors than a brunette or blonde, will be less at risk for diabetes and arthritis, among other things.

Redhead kids are inarguably the cutest.

 I'm not holding a vote or putting this in a poll, because have you seen photos of ginger babies? We look like tiny mer-people, but without the fish tails. Our eyes sparkle just a little bit more, and it goes without saying that our curls and waves of hair are a direct indicator that miracles happen. It's just an undeniable truth that your red child will be significantly cuter, and it's a burden we know you can handle.

#1 RED

THE *DOS* AND *DON'TS* OF RAISING A RED

Despite the fact that someone paid me to write this book, I'm not actually a child psychologist. (I know, it's confusing, because aren't all books written by PhDs?) But what's more important is that I'm a Secret Society of Redheads member, and what I know is that you'll want to tailor your parenting methods to the very specific needs of your ginge. Especially since they'll experience situations you may have zero understanding of or simply don't remember. Luckily, there are tips to use from when they're babies all the way up until they leave the house.

SITUATION: Your ginge wants to go outside. Gasp!

DO: Make sure they apply sunblock to all of their exposed skin (we're more prone to burns, and we don't want those little ginges to get skin cancer down the line!), and encourage them to wear hats because, ya know, sunburns again.

DON'T: Tell them they can't go outside or make them so afraid of burns that they never take off their clothes, including indoors. Some people (cough, cough: my mom) can get a little aggressive with the warnings and not consider that they're basically forcing their child into therapy as a result.

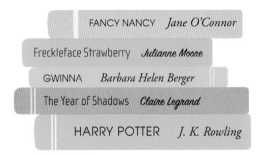

BOOKS TO READ TO YOUR RED

FANCY NANCY *Jane O'Connor*

Freckleface Strawberry *Julianne Moore*

GWINNA *Barbara Helen Berger*

The Year of Shadows *Claire Legrand*

HARRY POTTER *J. K. Rowling*

SITUATION: *Some jerk-for-brains makes fun of your kid's hair. Jerks, right?*

DO: Immediately put the kibosh on the idea that their hair is anything other than magnificent. Even if your kid isn't feeling supported at school, the fact that you always have their back and are their biggest cheerleader will be the most important thing.

DON'T: Beat the other kid up, even though you'll be super tempted.

SITUATION: *You have to give your ginge the ol' "birds and the bees" talk.*

DO: Remember to talk to them not just about the normal sex stuff but the more redhead-specific stuff. For girls, you'll want to address the fact that because of their hair color, people might make certain assumptions about them. Like, that they're going to be crazier about sex. For better or worse, these assumptions exist, but it's not something they should ever feel pressured to conform to (unless they want to, of course).

DON'T: Make the sex talk an experience they'll have to relive in therapy, please.

SITUATION: Someone tries to touch your ginge's hair.

DO: Hulk out and feel free to step in front of your child to physically block that person from having access to your kid.

DON'T: Feel obligated to let someone touch your kid's hair. It's their body and their hair and there's no reason to let someone else violate their personal space. People don't realize how isolating it can be to single someone out for a physical trait, so don't feel bad about going alpha parent and telling them to step off.

SITUATION: Someone tells your kid they have no soul.

DO: Roll your eyes. It's OK to make light of this one, if only because it's so inane. And you can remind them what a silly thing this is by helping them to laugh it off too. Obviously, we have souls. In fact, we likely gave the rest of the world a soul just by allowing them the gift of looking at us. If your kid is feeling really bad, remind them that if they have no soul, they get to live forever, which is a pretty good consolation prize.

DON'T: Forget to train them to create a new identity so that when they *do* live forever, they can start a new life every hundred years or so. Wait . . . who said that?!

SITUATION: *Your teenage ginge is upset about not being able to get a tan.* #thestruggle

DO: Sympathize, because there will be certain points in every red's life when they wish they could be like everyone else. But then cut the sympathy and point them to the self-tanners.

DON'T: Ever let them try a tanning bed. Like, ever.

SITUATION: *Your little red hates their hair.*

DO: Always tell your child how unique and special they are. Make a big freaking deal of it. Most reds go through a phase where they hate the color of their hair because it makes them a target. But encourage them to dress as their favorite ginger-haired heroes and make sure they're surrounded as much as possible by things that will make them feel included.

DON'T: Forget to remind them of this moment when they're in their twenties so they can have a good LOL about how silly they sounded.

The Problem with Barbie

When I was a little kid, dolls were like currency. And more specifically, the $100 bill of dolls was Barbie. My friends and I would compare Barbie accessories, discuss who had the newest version of the Dream House, and play with our dolls for tens of minutes before trying to trade them. I needed them all: Glitter Hair Barbie, Caboodles Barbie, and the ultimate: the My Size Barbie. It wasn't unlike a Barbie black market, and in my seven-year-old brain, the stakes felt pretty equal to selling a kidney.

But it was when I turned eight that my mom came home with a new doll for my birthday. A non-Barbie doll. It looked very different from what I'd grown accustomed to. For one thing, she was missing an eye. And the one good eye that remained was permanently stuck open with a thickly painted-on black iris and pupil, not unlike a shark. Her skin was porcelain—the material and the color—and I was told it was an antique. She also had red hair. When I tried to protest—it reminded me of a toy I'd just read about in one of my *Goosebumps* books—my mom firmly planted it on my dresser. Within a week there was another antique redhead doll because, as my mom explained, they were far more beautiful and expensive than some plastic Barbie. It wasn't long before my dresser was lined with them. Little redhead girls in tattered gingham gowns, with accessories like a teakettle or a broom. There was even one doll that appeared to be holding a dead mouse, though my mom insisted it was alive. Not that that fact made it any better.

My room quickly turned into one giant showroom for the redhead dolls, while my mom installed a shelf high in my closet to store the Barbies I'd worked so hard to collect. I wasn't happy, and for better or worse, I was inundated with antique doll gingers that were most certainly haunted and watching me sleep. When I woke up, they stared unblinkingly back. When I went to play with a toy, it was the antiques I could reach, not the Barbies. It was sort of like looking into a cupboard and seeing the sugary cookies all the way at the top, but the only things within reach were the carrots and hummus. Just torture. Eventually, they grew on me. After all, I didn't really have any other options. And I can distinctly remember comparing my own hair color to theirs, getting very excited when they nearly matched up. That never happened with Barbie. So, hey, maybe they weren't so bad after all . . .

My mom was trying to make up for the fact that Barbie didn't come with red hair—I realize that now. At the time, it felt like a special form of punishment, but now I know that she didn't want me idolizing Barbie, a doll that looked nothing like me, because that would never be who I was. As a little ginger I was already an outsider, and the fact that nothing in my environment made me feel included wasn't lost on my mother. So she did what she could and improvised with the antique dolls, which gave me a boost of self-esteem. Even though one of these dolls was most definitely a mouse murderer.

eight

How to Treat a Ginger

You'll Only Truly Understand If You're a Real, Live Red

N ot everything can be taught. And while this book can help norms begin to wrap their heads around the lives of redheads, there's only one true way to know what we're all about: to be one of us. This chapter should just feel like one big group hug. Or, if you hate hugs, it'll be like the best slice of pie you've ever had. Because one of the more frustrating aspects of being ginger is that unmistakable feeling that no one really understands you. And what I'm here to tell you is that I get it, and many other reds get it too. So we're going to put everything on the table. We'll go over scenarios that all redheads have to face, and we'll discuss the more distasteful things norms say so we can get that off our chests. It's time that we all embrace that #redheadlife, and this section is a great launching pad.

THINGS TO *AVOID* SAYING TO A REDHEAD

Fun Fact: [*] No Doubt's iconic "Don't Speak" was actually written for redheads to sing to the norms whenever they say things they shouldn't. Just . . . don't speak, norms. You've said more than enough. And yet norms still don't seem to understand that what they're saying can often be hurtful and borderline offensive. Sure, reds have an amazing sense of humor, but there are some phrases that just go too far. We've all heard at least one of these, so it's time to lay out what's unacceptable so that the norms learn something for once in their lives.

1. *"Are you allowed in the sun?"*

WHY YOU SHOULD AVOID IT: This comment implies that if we go in the sun, we'll instantly turn to dust. Which harkens back to the myth that we're all vampires. Admittedly, we reds should avoid too much exposure to the sun at all costs, but don't tell us how to live our lives. The fashion gods invented sun hats for a reason, after all.

HOW TO RESPOND TO IT: If you feel like being a little cheeky, a simple "I can't go in the sun. I have an ankle bracelet that beeps if I try," will do.

---

[*] I use the word "fact" loosely. It's a fact in my mind, at least.

2. "What's it like to not have a soul?"

WHY IT SHOULD BE AVOIDED: This is just offensive. Sure, we look like mythical creatures but spiritually we're just the same as everyone else (well, mostly the same). And even if we don't have souls, how is that any of your damn business?

HOW TO RESPOND TO IT: "It sucks, and now I'm about to steal yours," should make them run away quickly.

3. "Haven't you ever wanted to dye your hair?"

WHY IT SHOULD BE AVOIDED: Asking us if we want to dye our hair suggests that there's something wrong with the color we have. Which, as we all know, is just plain wrong. We redheads take enormous pride in our hair. Even if we hate it a little when we're younger, by the time we're sane adults, we realize just how incredibly lucky we are to have it. So don't assume we'd ever color it, and don't imply you'd want to change us.

HOW TO RESPOND TO IT: Feel free to kick this comment to the curb with "I would never dye my hair. But if you want to copy my color, I can send pics to your stylist."

4. "Is it red . . . down there?"

WHY IT SHOULD BE AVOIDED: Come on, sheeple. You're better than this comment! You're above asking us about our pubic hair, aren't you? And you already know the answer to this: yes, our bewitching pubes are red. We know that can be confusing and cause new feelings in your nether parts, but don't take your sexual curiosity out on us. Plus, if you ask us this question, you'll never get the chance to see the answer for yourself.

HOW TO RESPOND TO IT: If someone takes the liberty to poke around your most private of parts, then you get the opportunity to put them in their place. "You're deeply disturbed." "I'd show you, but seven days after you see it you'll die."

5. "I've never had sex with a redhead before."

WHY IT SHOULD BE AVOIDED: It's not totally clear what people think will happen when they say this. What could we possibly respond with other than "You need psychological help"? Maybe it all goes back to the whole vixen thing, that we're something to be ticked off on a list of "people to do," or maybe some people just think it's a legitimate pickup line. Either way, it won't end well if you say it.

HOW TO RESPOND TO IT: Condoning physical violence is wrong, but if you have a glass of wine handy, feel free to throw it in that person's face. Otherwise, "And now you never will sleep with a redhead," should solve this.

6. "You're a redheaded stepchild."

WHY IT SHOULD BE AVOIDED: While it may seem like a funny thing to say when you want to get a rise out of us, it's essentially suggesting we're unwanted. And as we've all learned, that's just false. Everyone wants us. And if someone says they don't want us, it just means they're afraid we'd reject them (we probably would, tbh).

HOW TO RESPOND TO IT: If they call you a redheaded stepchild, then the door is open for you to call them a terrible excuse for a human.

> ### THINGS TO SAY TO FLATTER A REDHEAD
>
> 1. "Your hair is positively inspiring me today."
> 2. "Do you think the universe created red hair so that when the apocalypse comes we'll all still have something beautiful to look at?"
> 3. "I'm thinking of funding a study based on my theory that all redheads are smarter than the rest of the population."
> 4. "Is it true that Amy Adams decided to dye her hair red after seeing a high school photo of you?"

When to Take a Stand

We all have that fantasy of slapping someone in the face, throwing a big glass of wine, or flipping a table onto our arch nemesis and walking out of the room with Beyoncé's "Sorry" playing in the background. The scenarios go deliciously on, but the biggest part of that fantasy is being able to react to someone in a way that lets them know you're DONE with this conversation.

For me, my moment came at a bar in Los Angeles called Happy Endings. The kind of respectable establishment where peanut shells and spilled beer congealed on the floor to the point where it no longer stuck to your shoes. I was there because I was chronically single. As in, I couldn't find anyone to make out with me, ever. I was pretty cute, had a job, and knew how to make the perfect microwaveable mac and cheese— so, ya know, a real catch—but I wasn't the most outgoing person. Like, I didn't enjoy most people. For example, I'd spent the prior weekend locked in my room binge-watching the first few seasons of *Lost*. Alone. And I was perfectly happy with that. But a *Lost* marathon wasn't exactly bringing the boys to my yard. So I reasoned that the only way to find real make-out friends was to put myself in locations where I could potentially bump into other warm bodies.

I'd dragged a few friends to Happy Endings too, and we spent two solid hours drinking cheap whiskey and trying to make eye contact with anyone who would have us. We'd given it a real desperate try, but no one was approaching. And like any woman who just wants to get back to watching her stories, I knew it was time to call it a night. So I went to close my tab, belly full of cheap liquor, and my heart yearning to be in pajamas. That's when I met him: a man with one elbow propped on the bar and a *Family Guy* tee that was about one size too small. "Hey," he said, and tapped me on the shoulder. I stepped aside, assuming I was blocking his way, but he stayed where he was and looked me up and down, the same way my cat checks out the whole of her food bowl before deciding which part to eat first. "I bet you're red everywhere, huh?" he said. Some friends behind him chuckled, or maybe they weren't his friends, but they certainly seemed to be on Team Jerkdog. "Are you serious?" I said. My voice came out much deeper and angrier than I'd intended, like the roar of a spirit who just discovered the Ghostbusters had been called. And maybe it was my newly booming voice, or the booze, but I took a step toward him. He backed up, hands in the air in surrender, "Didn't mean to offend," he said. But he did mean to offend, and I was having none of it.

I'd brought the watery remains of my last drink up to the bar, and I turned to grab the glass. I had it all set: I'd throw the drink in his face, watch him cower, and walk away dragging my friends with me. I'd be a hero, likely awarded a prize from the mayor for taking down the scum of the city. Which is why I was so acutely dismayed when I went to throw the drink and tripped over my own heel instead. I tumbled forward, as did my glass, and it landed just a few inches short of the offender's dirty sneakers. While I didn't totally get to live out my fantasy moment, I do think he got the point: don't insult a redhead, or else we'll trip and potentially take you down with us.

LET'S TALK ABOUT *BULLYING*

If given the choice between getting in a fight or, say, having a nice long sit with some pretzel bites, none of us would ever choose the former. But as a redhead, we all know that getting mocked for our hair is an unfortunate reality. And it doesn't really matter what age you are—it happens in school, but it can also happen in adulthood (like, I still hear "firecrotch" from time to time, and people accuse me of having a fiery temper on the regular). As a result, we've all dreamed of burning everyone to the ground à la Daenerys in *Game of Thrones*. But since most of us don't have access to dragons, we've got to figure out other ways to deal. Because while bullying for gingers is often at its worst when we're kids, it doesn't end the minute you become an adult. That bullying morphs into microaggressions and nicknames, becoming something so subtle that it's often hard to pinpoint. But the important thing is that we're in this together. As a red, you're never alone in the experience of being singled out for your ginger mane. So let's just talk about it together, because if there's one thing we can all understand, it's how it feels to be "different."

REDHEAD SECRET:
What doesn't kill us
makes us redder.

THE BIG REDHEAD BOOK

WHERE KICK A GINGER DAY CAME FROM

Since we know that the media plays such an influential role in how we're perceived, it only seems fair to start by addressing the elephant in the room. That elephant, of course, is season 9, episode 11, of *South Park*: "Ginger Kids."

Maybe you've seen it or maybe you haven't, but let me give you a refresher: in the episode, Cartman delivers a presentation to his class about a disease called "gingervitis." Gingervitis, according to Cartman, "causes very light skin, red hair, and freckles" and happens naturally because "ginger kids have no souls." He compares reds to vampires, calls the ginger gene a curse, and encourages the class to rid the earth of redheads. He also coins the term "daywalkers" (i.e., people with red hair who don't have freckles). The entire episode is a clear nod to what can happen when you single a group out for the way they look. And the surrounding characters speak to that point, with Kyle pointing out that Cartman's speech is "not a presentation; it's a hate speech." And Kyle, who happens to be a "daywalker," goes on to further question where this could lead: "Don't you understand what ignorant prejudice like that could lead to?"

The problem, however, is that the bigger issue of prejudice gets lost quickly in the episode. Rather than social commentary, which *South Park* is so often fantastic at, the episode devolves into a general bashing of red hair and the people who have it. "I, for one, hate ginger kids," Cartman's doctor says. "Sick!" "Gross!" and "Yuck!" Cartman exclaims as he sees photos of redhead kids. Visually, we also see an army of ginger kids attacking people, creeping into their homes, and in general, being particularly sinister and disturbing. The episode depicts all redheads as strange and evil, as there isn't a redeeming moment for them, and assumes the viewers will simply laugh that portrayal off. But for most redheads, watching the episode is like being on one of those old rickety wooden coasters. You're hopeful that this will be a fun ride, but then you hear the rusted hinges clanking against the side of the car, and your frayed seat belt starts to come loose, and you can't help thinking, "I've made a huge mistake." The "Ginger Kids" episode gives you a sinking in your gut, and when you're finished watching, instead of leaving with a sense of *Wow, never thought about it like that*, you're left with a feeling of *Oh, that was really fucking weird and hurtful.* Some reds may have found it funny, but the reds I've spoken to didn't. And it can be hard to try and describe to the norms exactly why the episode makes you a little uneasy—you don't want to seem like you can't take a joke, but at the same time it feels like the episode pushes everything past the point of a joke.

To further that, some fans of the show didn't view it entirely as a joke either. Because this episode of *South Park* single-handedly launched the start of an unofficial holiday called Kick a Ginger Day. The idea being that every year there's a day where you're encouraged to kick any redheads you see. There's even a Web site dedicated to the holiday (it's kick-a-ginger-day.com, if you feel the need to be filled with rage), which cites *South Park* as its inspiration. "As a JOKE, fans of the show have created the event 'Kick a Ginger Day,'" the site boasts, "mostly because the show does deliver a very compelling and humorous argument against redheads (that they have no souls)." Those who currently run the site insist that this is a joke holiday and that no reds should truly be kicked. But in the real world, this "joke" has inspired actual violence against reds.

It all began in 2008 when a fourteen-year-old Canadian boy launched a Facebook page called "Kick a Ginger," inspired by the episode. The group actually encouraged its five thousand members to inflict violence on redheads, stating that they should "get them steel toes ready."[35] And on November 20, 2008, many of the group's members carried out that message. In British Columbia, one thirteen-year-old boy reported being assaulted eighty times[36] that day, and twenty students were suspended from a Vancouver Island

ON NOVEMBER 20, 2008, A THIRTEEN-YEAR-OLD BOY WAS ASSAULTED EIGHTY TIMES.

middle school for participating.[37] After the initial acts of violence, a police spokeswoman was quoted as saying, "This is sort of inciting hate. It's a hate crime, really." In 2009, a school in Calabasas, California, (home of the Kardashians, if that place at all sounds familiar) reported a slew of attacks prompted by the holiday, along with three arrests of students for assault.[38] Then in 2013, parents from a school in England set up a Facebook group to discuss the attacks their children had suffered after students celebrated Kick a Ginger Day.[39] And in 2015, the *Daily Mail* reported that multiple students were attacked at a middle school in Massachusetts. These are just a few examples of the crimes committed as a result of this "joke" holiday. Makes you want to hug the nearest ginger you can find, right?

And while the *South Park* episode was definitely the first time reds were used to get a message across about prejudice, it wasn't the last. In 2010, singer M.I.A. released the video for her song, "Born Free." In the video, redheaded men are rounded up by police, thrown onto a bus, and led into the desert, where a redhead genocide occurs. The video is graphic and incredibly violent, but also serves as commentary on how minorities are often treated. But unlike the "Ginger Kids" episode, M.I.A.'s video actually does get a powerful message across. It makes you question why we think it's OK to view certain groups of people as the "other" and what consequences doing so has on those people. And the violence highlights the senselessness that so many groups face just because of their physical appearance. To my knowledge, no violence against redheads occurred after the release of the music video, which suggests that M.I.A's message went right, whereas *South Park*'s went wrong.

> ## IN 2012, A FOURTEEN-YEAR-OLD BOY COMMITTED SUICIDE AFTER BEING TEASED RELENTLESSLY FOR HAVING RED HAIR.

That doesn't make M.I.A.'s video any easier to watch as a redhead, though. Because when you already feel like a kind of "other" in your everyday life, to see that dramatized on-screen just brutally points out what you already know: people think you're different. The redhead boys are being rounded up as a result of how they look. But because we're simply a group of people with the same hair color, it makes talking about these situations a bit more complicated. After all, if it's just a hair color, then what's the big deal, right? It is a type of discrimination though, because we've certainly been labeled, ridiculed, and brutalized as a result of how we look. And the bullying that happens to redheads should be taken seriously, because to underestimate the effect it can have on a person is dangerous. For example, in 2012 a fourteen-year-old boy named Simon Walters committed suicide after being relentlessly teased for having red hair.[40] According to the boy's father, they'd alerted school officials, and Simon had even dyed his hair brown in an effort to stop the torment. And in 2013, in a very similar story, fifteen-year-old Helena Farrell committed suicide, and her father reported that she might still be alive if she hadn't been so continuously bullied over her red hair.[41] Mr. Farrell took things a step further when, after his daughter's death, he called for lawmakers to make it illegal to discriminate against someone with red hair. There was even an entire family in England that was forced to move multiple times as a result of bullying due to their hair color—and the father alleged that they'd simply been told to dye their hair if they wanted the bullying to stop.[42]

It's fair to say that most redheads have experienced some kind of bullying as a result of how they look. And in the extreme cases, like those above, it can destroy lives. It's just something for the norms reading this to think about: words have impact, and just because you think teasing redheads is a joke doesn't mean it's actually funny.

SO, WHY DO BULLIES THINK THIS IS OK?

Now I'm not going to focus on the fact that bullying is awful, because we all know that to be true. But we will talk about why bullying happens in the first place. Because once we know the motives and can see past the bullies and into their very souls, it's a lot easier to get on with bigger and redder things. (Spoiler alert: most bullies are just insecure sad sacks.) So, why do bullies love that **#bullylife** so very much?

This may sound corny AF, but people bully when they're jealous. And oftentimes when people are jealous of something and know they can't have it, they try to destroy it. For example, when my brother and I were little, I remember one night we were fighting over a jump rope. I know, we were basic as hell, but we both loved that thing. And our babysitter asked whose it was. It was my brother's, but I wanted it, so we both said it was ours. And when she threatened to throw it out unless we told the truth, I told her to go ahead, toss it, I didn't care. The truth was that I just didn't want my brother to have it, because I couldn't have it. When our sitter saw my brother sobbing, she knew it was his and rightfully gave it back to him while I sulked in time-out. And it's the same deal with bullies: they can't handle their jealousy over our gorgeous hair, so they try and destroy it with insults. Just remember that jealousy is a disease, so let's pray these norms get well soon.

We reds have a visual marker on our heads that tells people there's something different about us. Admittedly, it's a beautiful marker, but it's still an indicator of that "otherness." We stand out in a crowd, and when someone is itching to bully, they'll look for the easiest target. Our hair is definitely easy to spot, and since there aren't a lot of folks with red hair, we often end up being singled out.

I'd probably give the same advice that my mom gave me, which is to hang in there. And just know that the kids picking on you are picking on you because you're different and they're maybe even a little jealous. So just understand that you're special, and you're unique, and you're beautiful being a redhead.

DARBY STANCHFIELD,
SCANDAL, *IN CONVERSATION WITH ME*

 People are afraid of things that are different, and all kinds of differences can lead to bullying. But since we're talking about reds, that's what we'll focus on here. Our difference is that we look like a glitch in the Matrix. One minute you're seeing an endless horizon of neutral colors and then, whoops, a fiery red blip floats across your screen. And since a lot of people are dumb-dumbs, their reaction to this shift is to assume the person with red hair is strange, dangerous, or a weirdo. So they make fun of you for being all of those things, even if you aren't, because it makes the norms feel safer. But imho, I'd rather be the weirdo any day.

> *The reason you're being bullied is because the bullies are definitely jealous of you. There's something about you that makes them uncomfortable because they don't have it. They feel uncomfortable because there's something "other" about you. And they feel the need to knock you down because they're threatened by whatever it is that's special about you.*
>
> ALICIA WITT,
> NASHVILLE AND JUSTIFIED,
> IN CONVERSATION WITH ME

Bullies sometimes bully for the simple reason that they're mean. People have all kinds of issues that they act out in various ways, and bullies release their own anger by belittling us, the reds. Maybe they're insecure, or having problems at home—whatever the reason, it makes them feel better to try and knock you down to their level.

REDHEAD SECRET:
Being bullied makes us much more tolerant people, and that's a good thing!

1. Magical Unicorn
2. The Two Percent
3. Hot Like Fire
4. Living Rainbow

 The only silver lining to this is that the experience of bullying can make you a much more tolerant person. Because when you're singled out, you don't want to inflict that on other people. And since you're viewed as an "other," you have empathy for those who are also looked at as being different. It's definitely a painful way to get to a more enlightened place, but many reds are more caring and understanding because of being bullied.

WEIRD MICROAGGRESSIONS ONLY REDHEADS HEAR

"I'm just not attracted to redheads."

"You're pretty . . . . for a redhead."

"Wait, you aren't Irish?"

"You don't look like a normal redhead."

"I know not to make you mad."

How to Treat a Ginger

nine

The Secret Society of Redheads

It's Time to Join Up!

I'm not talking about us all uniting in a cult, starting a ginger religion, or even a red revolution, although, now that I mention it . . . It would just be really incredible if we could have even more redhead solidarity than we already do. In the opening of this book, I talked about the Gingers Unite sighting, which is when you see a redhead you don't know out in the wild and give them a look that says, "I understand you." That's a form of solidarity right there, and it's probably the simplest act of camaraderie we have, and yet for many reds that kind of commonality takes a long time to find. I'm included in that group. Throughout my teens I'd grown accustomed to being the only ginger in a room, so I'd often feel threatened when I encountered another red. *There can only be one of us*, I told myself in a menacing voice. And I know I'm not the only red who's acted this way—so many of us spend our lives being possessive of our hair color, because it's exactly what makes us feel unique. So to see someone else with it can lead to a "I don't want to share my special hair with you" mentality.

But here's the thing: there's power in redheads coming together. It's totally natural to be uneasy about someone stealing your hair thunder. It's your hair, not theirs! Except it is theirs and yours, and the sooner we all learn to unite together as reds, the more support we'll have. While we're all individual people, we're also unmistakably linked by our everyday experiences. And now that we've found each other through this book, let's celebrate the whole not-being-alone thing. We're part of one enormous Secret Society of Redheads, and as redheads it's our duty to celebrate each other. We'll always have our bond, and that's probably the very best part of being ginger.

I like having hair that looks
like a volcano is erupting.
It's kind of dramatic.

ACTRESS KAREN GILLAN,
DOCTOR WHO AND
GUARDIANS OF THE GALAXY,
IN CONVERSATION WITH ME

Making Your First Real Redhead Friend (RRF)

When I was twenty-three years old I moved to Los Angeles and got a job as an assistant at an agency (think Lloyd from *Entourage*, but on a much smaller scale). And after my first week, I was 100 percent certain I was about to get fired. I had two bosses who were both extremely particular and demanding—one needed me to make his coffee *just* right, while the other one liked to test me by asking things like, "Who called me at 11:04 yesterday?" I just wasn't very good at that job, and they both knew it. But I also had to keep that job so I could do things like pay rent and eat food that didn't exclusively come from a can. And I saw a ray of hope in the other assistant in my office, Tom.

Tom was intimidating in that he was perfect at his job, always wore color-block cardigans, and was a flaming redhead just like me. And while I'd usually try to shoot laser beams out of my eyes to communicate there could ONLY BE ONE of us, I really needed him to be my friend. He'd been an assistant for a few years and knew how to wrangle my bosses. He was the only one who could help me not get fired and not eat beans for the rest of my life. But for whatever reason, he kept going out of his way to ignore me. So I did what any desperate person would: I complimented the shit out of him every day and bought him coffee until he finally caved. It took weeks, but he started being nice and giving me tips, "See what you just did? Do the opposite." He trained me to be a better assistant, and I managed to keep my job.

About a month later, Tom confessed that he'd initially suffered the same thing I had: redhead envy. He didn't exactly

Continued on next page

Continued from previous page

love that there was another one of us in the office. He was used to being the special redhead there, and he refused to acknowledge my existence as a result. But soon after he'd let go of that, we were able to talk, make each other laugh, and again: talk. In fact, once we started talking, we couldn't stop, and it was all about redhead things. We'd walk down the street to the coffee shop, and the barista would ask if we were siblings. "Does that happen anytime you're in a room with another redhead?" he asked. "Yes!" I practically screamed. We'd had so many of the same experiences with dating, growing up, and self-confidence (or lack thereof) that we made a blog about being redheads together. (Google "Oh Shit! I'm A Ginger" if you want to see this work of art).

The best part of making my first real redhead friend was that I was finally able to express so many of the things that had frustrated me throughout my life, and he totally understood. Like, what are boys even, and why aren't they all interested in dating redheads?! By talking things out with Tom, we both came to understand that, while there were a lot of annoying ginger moments, we both genuinely loved our red color. It was part of us, and we wouldn't change it, even though we both regularly got catcalled for our hair while walking down the street. Instead, we started to like our tinge of ginge more and appreciated the fact that we weren't alone in our redhead journey. Whenever we hung out, we celebrated our redheadedness together. And in that way, Tom really helped me (and vice versa) become a better red.

HOW *BIG* OF A GINGER ARE YOU?

If you have red hair, then you're a ginger. Contest over: you're the winner! But there are levels to being a redhead, and certain life milestones that help get you closer and closer to being an ULTIMATE red. In the same way that paying taxes brings you further into adulthood, having someone tell you they have a "thing for redheads" makes you a higher-level ginger. Maybe not each and every one of these will apply, but when you have that gut-check of, "Ah, yes, that happened to me," then just know we're all right there with ya. As you go through everything below, check off all the things you've personally experienced as a redhead, and see how much of a ginger you truly are.

REDHEAD SECRET:
We all get called "red," and we never forget who called us that.

Check off all that apply:

YOU'VE BEEN CALLED "RED," "BIG RED," "GINGER," OR ANOTHER REDHEAD-RELATED NICKNAME INSTEAD OF YOUR ACTUAL NAME.

Real talk: Sometimes this is OK—like maybe you both have nicknames for each other, so it's more endearing and less cry-me-a-river. If you fall into that camp, then hooray! However, if your nickname makes you wonder, "Does this person even know my real name?" then it's time to stop the bullshit. And perhaps the most effective way to do that is to mirror back what the person is saying. So when someone asks, "Hey Red, got a minute?" you'd respond with, "Yeah, Blondie, I do." You can sub in curly, brunette, baldie, or whatever else their hair type is. Chances are they won't like it very much either and will get the subtle hint.

YOU'VE BEEN OUT WITH ANOTHER REDHEAD AND SOMEONE ASKED IF YOU TWO WERE RELATED.

Real talk: If you have a red friend, you're going to get mistaken for being related. It all goes back to how scarce we are, and people just assume that we'd never be able to find one another without sharing a bloodline. It also might happen when you're at a party and another random red is there. It will happen, if it hasn't already, and whether or not you want to call a person out for it is totally up to you.

THE BIG REDHEAD BOOK

YOU'VE HEARD THE SENTENCE, "DO YOU KNOW MY FRIEND [INSERT NAME HERE]? THEY'RE A REDHEAD TOO."

Real talk: For norms, they assume we're all sister-wives and in contact with each other at all times. And while it's true that we're all in the Secret Society of Redheads, there are just far too many of us to keep track of. (Well, at least without the help of our handy ginger directory.) So pull a Mariah Carey and say, "I don't know her," because chances are you don't.

 YOU'VE WANTED TO DYE YOUR HAIR AND BEEN TOLD NOT TO.

Real talk: Some reds have never dyed their hair; some have. But if you really want to, then just go out and dye away. You gotta do you. Just don't be surprised if your hair stylist balks or even refuses to do it. And know that when you're ready to come back to the red side (and eventually you will be), we're all here and rooting for you.

 YOU'D RATHER HAVE ALL YOUR TEETH FALL OUT THAN GO TO THE DENTIST.

Real talk: It's scientifically proven that we require more anesthesia at the dentist, so dental anxiety is totally normal for reds! But know what can make this easier? Dental spas. A spa for your teeth and you, my reds! In addition to cleaning, they also offer things to distract you, like noise-canceling headphones, flat-screen TVs, and massage treatments. Or, ya know, just let your teeth fall out.*

---

* Kidding . . . kind of.

SOMEONE HAS SAID, "IT'S KISS A GINGER DAY" AND EXPECTED A KISS.

Real talk: Look, if Dwayne "the Rock" Johnson says it's Kiss a Ginger Day and he wants to celebrate, then who among us would object? But more likely than not, you'll be informed of the holiday (which is on January 12) by someone less pleasant, someone who isn't the Rock. And that's where the problems come in. This "holiday" was created after Kick a Ginger Day popped up to try and counteract the bullying with a more "positive" experience. And if you're totally down for it, or the Rock shows up, then lean in, my red friend. If, however, you'd rather not pucker up just because you're ginger, then spend the day at home curled up on a couch with your life partner, Netflix.

YOU'VE MET SOMEONE WITH A REDHEAD FETISH.

Real talk: Like restaurants that serve mac-and-cheese burgers, things that are rare tend to get a following. People who like that rare thing aren't always able to find it, so they start thinking of it as something they need to have, want to be part of, and would do just about anything to get. Essentially, someone who has a redhead fetish knows a good thing when they see it. And there is a spectrum of redhead fetishes—some simply find the color attractive, while others may try to date only redheads because they have a "thing" for them. Either way, it means you've got someone in your life who deeply appreciates what you have to offer. (Not a bad thing!) Just keep in mind that, as with any fetish, the person is viewing the thing they desire (your hair) as an object. So if you decide to try a serious relationship with a redhead fetishist, make sure they're invested in the whole package, and not just the hair bit.

BABIES AND SMALL CHILDREN HAVE STARED AT YOUR HAIR FOR UNREASONABLY LONG PERIODS OF TIME.

Real talk: Maybe it's because babies are really stimulated by bright colors or you remind them of the animated characters they see on TV. But either way: kids tend to stare. It's definitely not in a "What is that thing?!" way, but they do seem mesmerized by red hair. Either way, you've got fans.

YOU'VE BEEN CATCALLED FOR YOUR HAIR.

Real talk: Ah, catcalling. That special time when you're minding your own business and get ambushed by a man who thinks it's OK to scream, "Let's see a smile, Red." What the hell is wrong with people?! And as a ginger it can feel doubly isolating because they choose your hair, the thing you love most, to try and take from you. But to quote Bianca Del Rio from *RuPaul's Drag Race*, respond with "Not today, Satan, not today."

YOU'VE BEEN ACCUSED OF HAVING A FIERY TEMPER.

Real talk: Seriously, let's just acknowledge that this is so annoying. Because when someone says you have a "fiery temper," they're effectively shutting down whatever you said. They brush it to the side and make it less meaningful by blaming it on your hair. And someday in the near future, all of the redheads with a "fiery temper" will gather in one place to light a bonfire and burn an effigy of those who've made these false assumptions. Joking, of course . . . or am I?

PEOPLE ASSUME YOU'RE IRISH.

Real talk: Oh, people and their stereotypes: you have red hair and therefore know how to find the pot of gold at the end of the rainbow. Not that there's anything wrong with being Irish, but redheads come from all over. Hell, maybe you do know where that gold is (in which case, call me!), but as we've already covered: redheads come from all over the world. You might be thinking, "Well, I should punch them in the face." And while that's a natural

REDHEAD SECRET:
We're not all Irish—we're alien! Kidding . . . kinda.

impulse, it's also one that could end up with any number of terrible outcomes, so I wouldn't recommend it. But that's just my opinion.

SOMEONE HAS ASKED IF YOU'RE A REAL REDHEAD.

Real talk: Reds get no R-E-D-S-P-E-C-T when it comes to keeping our secrets. While norms would likely never go up to a blond stranger and ask if they're natural or dye jobs, they seem to have no problem asking us. First of all, your natural hair color is no one's business. And even if you are a dyed ginger, that just means you chose the more vibrant side of life. (Welcome to our society.)

THE BIG REDHEAD BOOK

SIX GINGER *MANTRAS* WE ALL NEED

We all get by with a little help from something. For some people, it's coffee; for others, it's Snapchats of cats—and if you're a redhead, you can go ahead and add these mantras to make your ginger life even better. A mantra can be something you say in your head or out loud for a few minutes every day, or something you pin to a wall as a reminder. And the great thing about a mantra is that it can empower you and bring you back to a good place whenever you're feeling a little less than. As we all know, redheads are borderline demigods, so we've got to keep our strength up at all times.

REDHEAD SECRET:
We have Julianne
Moore on our side.

1. *"Julianne Moore has my back."* She does. She loves being a redhead. She wrote a book about having ginger locks called *Freckleface Strawberry* and has said, "There's a great feeling of solidarity that we have, as freckly redheads . . . I'll smile at a redhead on the street, and they'll smile back."

2. *"People make fun of my hair because they can never, ever have my hair."* As a redhead, you're not better than anyone else, but people assume you might be. And they're coveting something that they can never get. So being the sad sacks they are, they'll try to

bring you down. And while this knowledge doesn't change the fact that you've been teased, it provides some perspective and maybe even encourages empathy, because not everyone can be as **#blessed** as you.

3. "I am a red, and therefore fearless AF." Not to stereotype, but we are, on average, bigger badasses than the norms. Because of our hair color, we endure a lot of bullying, side looks, and the occasional hair touching from strangers. Which means the older we get, the more likely we are to be fearless. We've seen some shit, and as a result we aren't about to sweat the small stuff.

> *When I was a kid I remember praying for my hair to turn brown. I thought it would help me in life to have "normal" hair. Perhaps even hair that people deemed "attractive." I think as I began to grow up and reached the age of fifteen, I'd accepted my ginger-ness wasn't going anywhere. I think true and full appreciation set in when I moved to London. I was seventeen and I started getting a lot of attention for the color of my hair. It was then that I thought . . . I could get used to this.*
>
> ACTRESS KAREN GILLAN,
> TO ME

4. "My hair is literally one of the colors of the rainbow." This is a fact. You're part of the ROYGBIV, and no one can take that away.

5. "Red is more." Sure, to be a norm and not get noticed as much would be a fine existence, but you're a red, and red is more. You don't need to change anything about who you are or what you look like, because the more you embrace that redness, the more likely you are to be confident in yourself and shine even brighter.

6. *"Redheads will one day inherit the earth."* Look, if the norms are right and we are soulless vampires, then it isn't the worst news for us. It means we'll outlive everyone else, and at the end of days, when the world has been wiped clean, it'll just be us with our solemn mission to repopulate the earth. Am I saying it'll be a pretty great time? Yes. And am I suggesting that this is a possibility for us? Absolutely. #TeamNoSoul

I think the great thing about redheads is that there are some stereotypes about our bad temper, or being the kids in band, or a really strong, complex person, but what I'd say that's really great is that there is an enigmatic quality. Redheads can do anything. They're hard to pin down. You can't just say "Oh, a redhead is one way."

ACTRESS DARBY STANCHFIELD, TO ME

HOW TO BE A BETTER RED

Even though we may have some complaints, reds are not so secretly in love with our hair. It's a borderline obsession, and we're not about to join a twelve-step program to get over it. There's always a way to make your everyday life better and redder. So whether you're a norm or a redhead, if you want to live your best red days, then there are some things to take into consideration.

TIP: Take a trip to a redhead convention. And if you didn't know those were a thing, then let me be the one to introduce you. Redhead Days is an organization that arranges redhead conventions across the world. Including one in the Netherlands, which is the largest annual redhead festival—a weekend each fall featuring all kinds of redhead-themed activities, like a fashion show, ginger contests, a pub crawl, and a whole slew of other things. Redhead Days also hosts a yearly convention in Chicago and another in London, among other places. So if you want to know what it feels like to be surrounded by redheads and be the majority for once, it's worth the trip.

> *I feel a kinship with redheads because I feel like they must have a similar experience. They probably went through something similar.*
>
> ACTRESS MARIA THAYER,
> *TO ME*

TIP: Choose a famous quote about redheads and memorize it, so you can spout it out like poetry whenever you need to. Mine is "Red hair is caused by sugar and lust," which is a quote from *Still Life with Woodpecker* by Tom Robbins. If you're in need of one, here are a few to snatch up:

✦ "Gingers earn a freckle for every soul they eat." —Unknown

✦ "Blondes are noticed, but redheads are never forgotten." —Unknown

✦ "Red hair is great. It's rare, and therefore superior." —Augusten Burroughs

REDHEAD SONGS TO ADD TO YOUR PLAYLIST

1. "Redhead Girl," by AIR
2. "Prejudice," by Tim Minchin
3. "Jolene," by Dolly Parton
4. "Redheaded Girl," by Tijuana Panthers
5. "Redhead Walking," by R.E.M.
6. "Red Headed Stranger," by Willie Nelson
7. "Pretty Redhead Girl," by MISTER
8. "Redhead Rosie," by the Fabulous Ginn Sisters
9. "Redhead Girl," by Weston
10. "The Band Played On," by John Palmer and Charles Ward
11. "Red Headed Woman," by Bruce Springsteen
12. "Valerie," by Amy Winehouse
13. "Tangled Up in Blue," by Bob Dylan
14. "Icky Thump," by the White Stripes
15. "1952 Vincent Black Lightning," by Richard Thompson
16. "Boot Scootin' Boogie" by Brooks and Dunn
17. "Ain't Goin Down ('Til the Sun Comes Up)," by Garth Brooks
18. "Good Time," by Counting Crows
19. "Cinnamon Girl," by Neil Young
20. "You Need Me, I Don't Need You," by Ed Sheeran

REX/Shutterstock.com

TIP: Don't be afraid to use the **#RedheadsUnite** hashtag in all of your social media platforms. It makes it a lot easier for us to find each other, and if you use it, I'll definitely give you a "follow" back and a "like." Do it for the "likes"!

TIP: Find a redhead icon to look up to if you don't already have one. This is especially important because, when you see references to that icon in pop culture, you can share them on your Facebook page and say, "My QUEEN!" making all of your followers question whether they should be worshipping your icon as well. Whoever they are, from Tori Amos to Bobby Flay to Julie Klausner, it's always good to have a redhead icon to model your life after.

TIP: Join a ginger Facebook group. Ginger Parrot, Redhead World, and We Are Redheads all have well-curated pages and feature articles about our hair, post photos of ginger families, and run discussion forums to talk about redhead things. If nothing else, it's a weird look inside other gingers' lives.

TIP: If you've got it, flaunt it. And by "it" I mean your red hair. Some reds' hair fades to white, and others lose it completely. But if you have it, then make sure you're highlighting that gorgeousness like a freshly frosted cake in a display window. People will look, and you may even convert some norms to the red side in the process.

BOOKS TO ADD TO YOUR BOOKSHELF

STILL LIFE WITH WOODPECKER   *Tom Robbins*   because both of the leads are redheads

MIDDLESEX   *Jeffrey Eugenides*   which discusses the beauty of red hair

RED: A HISTORY OF THE REDHEAD   *Jacky Colliss Harvey*   for when you need a deep-dive into red hair

The Roots of Desire   *Marion Roach*   because her interpretation of being ginger is fascinating

HOW TO BE A REDHEAD   *Adrienne and Stephanie Vendetti*   for when you need a guide on how to live your best redhead beauty life

ELEANOR & PARK   *Rainbow Rowell*   because Eleanor is called "Big Red" for her hair, and we can all relate to that

Harry Potter   *J. K. Rowling*   because we all need more Weasleys in our life

THE OUTLANDER SERIES   *Diana Gabaldon*   for a hot ginger man fix

Ed Sheeran ✔
@edsheeran

some people thought i would never become successful because of my hair colour, how mad is that!? idiots

Conan O'Brien ✔
@ConanOBrien

Ladies, let's just say that the carpet matches whatever the metaphor for back hair would be.

TIP: Follow all of the redhead celebs you can find on Twitter. A lot of times they'll tweet about their hair or redhead occurrences. It's just fun, really.

TIP: Acknowledge your fellow redheads when you see us out in the wild. If you haven't experienced the Gingers Unite acknowledgment IRL, then it's time to start doing it. If you're a norm, it's best not to nod and smile at all the reds you see unless you want to get some shifty looks. But if you're a red and see a fellow red, you've gotta own it. Smile, nod, say "nice hair" as you pass them. Just let them know you've got their back, and they'll have yours.

STEPS TO A GINGERS UNITE SIGHTING

Step 1: Spot your fellow red.

Step 2: Wait for fellow red to make eye contact.

Step 3: Choose your mode of acknowledgment: nod, "Hey, Red," smile, throwing rose petals at their feet.

THE BIG REDHEAD BOOK

TIP: Adopt a ginger pet. What? This one seems like too much of a stretch? Well, tell that to the ginger cat who just wants to cuddle and compare shades with you.

TIP: Stick up for your fellow redheads whenever the opportunity arises. And this is a tip that norms can assist with too! A coworker once offhandedly said her brother was acting, "like a redheaded stepchild." Once she remembered that I had a tinge of ginge she apologized for saying that, but I also told her that was a weird thing to say. I'm pretty sure she'll never resort to that turn of phrase again, and my job here is done.

TIP: Throw your money at any movies or TV shows with redhead leads. If we want more representation of reds in the media, then we need to show the people who make media that we support them. So if you see a TV show with a ginger lead or a film starring a redhead, make it your business to at least give it a shot. And if you're feeling extra generous, post about that thing on your Facebook—spread the word!

TIP: If a new redhead enters your part of the world, go out of your way to chat with them. Don't be like past me and adopt the "There can only be ONE OF US" attitude. That's no way to make ginger friends, and it certainly won't work out well for you in the long run. So go ahead, show some solidarity and always make a beeline for the red in the room. Your hair is basically a built-in conversation starter.

TIP: Get a ginger friend group going. This one is easier said than done, especially since reds can be scarce, but you can definitely make it happen. Don't have any red friends? Ask your current friend group if they have any, and if they'd be willing to set you up on a friend date. If you're at a party and see a red, approach them and see if they might be a FGF (Forever Ginger Friend). It can start out small (a party of two is still a party), and chances are that throughout the years you'll slowly add more to your circle until you have a small but mighty redhead contingent. You know, people you can go to see ginger movies with (I went to see *Brave* with my ginger buds), drink whiskey gingers around, or just meet to chat about your red lives. It'll be nice to have a support system of people you can deeply relate to, regardless.

RED SHOWS TO WATCH

REDFLIX

Unbreakable Kimmy Schmidt, for our naive hero
Scandal, for Abby and all of the ginger nicknames she receives
Six Feet Under, for Claire Fisher
Buffy the Vampire Slayer, for Oz and Willow
The Catch, for a seriously badass Mireille Enos
Dexter, to watch Michael C. Hall's hair get redder in the moonlight

Wolfgang van de Rydt/
Fantareis/Pixabay

ARE YOU RED-Y TO JOIN THE SSR
(SECRET SOCIETY OF REDHEADS)?

Secret Redhead Society, Redhead Coven, Group of Kickass Reds You Like to Eat Chocolate With . . . whatever you want to call it, it's time to join up. And I'd like to personally extend an invite for you to join the SSR. Membership is free, and the requirements are as follows:

✦ You're a natural redhead, or identify as "pro-red."

✦ You believe in life, liberty, and the pursuit of redness.

✦ You firmly feel that only gingers should call other gingers "ginger."

✦ You've never used the word "firecrotch" in a derogatory manner.

✦ And on that note, you've never asked a red if the carpet matches the drapes.

✦ You think Kick a Ginger Day is a plot by the norms to try and bring down the reds.

✦ But you also firmly know that reds can never be stymied.

✦ You know that redheads are magical unicorns.

That's it! Those are all the requirements for entry. No age limits, no entry fee, no judgments on your penchant for wearing sneakers to a club. And the benefits, you may be wondering? Well, you're part of that elusive 2 percent club, get acknowledgment from fellow reds, and are straight-up ON THE LIST for the rager we're gonna throw when the end of days comes. If you're a red,

> *I think we're in the secret club. The SPF club. We're all in it together. When you see each other you're like, "yeah, we wear long-sleeved shirts to the beach."*
>
> ACTOR CAMERON MONAGHAN, TO ME

then all you need to do is snap your fingers, open the society handbook (a.k.a. this book), and remind yourself of what a supernatural creature you truly are. And if you're a norm, then when you open this book, you'll know how truly blessed you are to be alive during a time when redheads are poised to rule the earth. Lucky all of us! As for official meetings, we hold those anytime we see one another. The secret code word is "Redheads Unite," and when you both say it out loud, it means you're in the presence of a fellow chosen one. At which point you both should head immediately to the nearest bar so you can drink and talk authoritatively about SSR-isms.

So if you want to take up the ginger cause, I'd like you to join me. We have a lot of work to do, and I'd love to have you by my red side. Let's share the information in this book with fellow reds and norms alike so they can begin to understand that they're basically walking among the gods. Share the fact that we can handle more physical pain than everyone else and have evolved to look like we don't even have gray hairs as we age. Open up dinner party conversations about the famous reds throughout history, and if you see a ginger being attacked in any way, stand up for them.

Now, if you're truly ready to live a life that's fully proginger, then it's time for you to take these sacred vows:

SSR VOWS

I, **[insert name here]**, do solemnly swear to be a proud and loyal member of the Secret Society of Redheads. It's a pretty big deal. I've pored through the pages of this book, and since reading a whole book is more than most people can say they've ever done, I'm actually a better person as a result. Basically, I've got a PhD in Gingerness.

As a member of the SSR, I will uphold the club's bylaws and the standards as set forth. When I see a fellow member, I'll acknowledge them and vow to be there if the time should come. And when I need to find my own personal strength, I'll just remember that redheads are literally better at tolerating pain than everyone else. We're like the Hulk, but less agro. And most important: I'll always know that being a redhead is a damn gift, not just for me, but for the world. I'll try not to be too pompous about that and go around demanding shit, even though I totally could. Like, it'd be awesome to have a throne in my living room for watching Netflix. But as I said, I'll hold back on the demands . . . for now.

When someone tries to bring me or my fellow redheads down, I'll respond by rising above their pettiness. And when something wonderful happens to a fellow redhead—like they have a ginger kid, or a movie gets a red lead—I'll help celebrate that success. As SSR members, we all know that redheads are fighters and have suffered through some pretty unfair things, but we're coming to a much better moment in history. It's our duty to embrace what's happening now, and always remember where we came from. Ashes to ashes, and dust to old stereotypes.

I will always be a proud SSR member and have my fellow reds' backs no matter what. **#RedheadsUnite**

Signed, a loyal Secret Society of Redheads member,
[insert signature below]

ACKNOWLEDGMENTS

I have written a lot of thank-you cards in my life, but it took me a long time to sort out where to start on the thank-yous for this book. Maybe it's best to begin with the first book I ever read about red hair, which was *The Roots of Desire* by Marion Roach. That book is single-handedly responsible for me feeling confident that I could write about red hair, and it sparked a bit of an obsession in me to find more answers. So a big thank-you to Roach, because her initial research and exploration was invaluable in the writing of this book. Speaking of invaluable help, *Red: A History of the Redhead* by Jacky Colliss Harvey is another incredible book about red hair that every red should read. Her exhaustive look into the history of red hair, the connotations it has, and how it led us all here also served as a major guide in my work. Did I mention that I reached out to both Roach and Harvey separately, told them about my book, and they both responded with redhead solidarity? Reds really are the best.

I don't think people who get interviewed for books or articles get enough credit, because they're essentially doing it for free, generously donating their time and expertise. And I interviewed a lot of people for this book. Some were famous reds like Darby Stanchfield, Cameron Monaghan, Alicia Witt, Karen Gillan, Daniel Newman, and Maria Thayer. While others were experts in their fields, like Thomas Knights, Professor Andrew Stott, Professor John T. Fitzgerald, and Dr. Helen Fisher. But all of them helped make this a fuller and more informed book, so I definitely owe them a drink the next time we meet.

Writing a book can be a superlonely process, mainly because you have to lock yourself in a room and write until your fingers fall off. But a lot of people helped keep me from tipping over the edge into Hermitville. Thank you to my incredible husband, Eoghan, who read every draft, gave me notes, and was my biggest support throughout the writing process. He also never complained about the fact that weekends were spent indoors for a solid seven months. Thank you, Eoghan, and thanks for being the absolute best human. My mom and dad let me call them as many times as I wanted when I needed a break from writing, as did my best friend, Elisa Atwell. And while we're at it, I had a lot of friends who just kept asking about the book and checking in the whole time, which made me feel really loved. Thank you, Amy Meyerson, Lynn Elias, Alex D'Italia, April Dávila, Lizzy Bradford, Tiffany Tran, Racheline Benveniste, Doriean Stevenson, Lucy Keating, Ghazal Moshfegh, Tom Farrell, and Hadi Deeb. Ashley Aruda and Chris Aragon were two people I would e-mail and ask, "Is this funny?" Then they'd tell me how to make it funnier, so basically any funny stuff is because they helped me through it.

The other thing about writing a book is that it takes a lot of time, and BuzzFeed—where I have a full-time job—was incredibly generous and let me take a book leave so I could write this. People like Tommy Wesely and Alex Naidus made sure that time was easy to take and that I didn't come back to a burning Dumpster fire. It's a really wonderful place to "work," and I put work in quotes because it never really feels like work. Thanks, BuzzFeed!

My agent, Kristyn Keene at ICM, believed in this book and me. Kristyn gave me the kind of notes and feedback I needed to hear, and she always made me feel like she had my back through the writing process. Plus, she's just a gem of a person. And Patrick Morley, also at ICM, was such a great help whenever I had questions or needed him to do some research. Then there's my editor, Jaime Coyne at St. Martin's Press. Can I even begin to thank her for all of the time she put into this book? Her notes were off-the-charts incredible, and I really feel that this book is better because of her careful eye. Thank you for loving redheads and everything about them, Jaime. And for that one time when you said a passage in this book was "fascinating," which made me feel like I'd hit a real home run.

I think having some key redheads in my life really made me want to write this book—in a lot of ways, I wrote it for them. My grandmother, Dorothy La Rosa, my brother Rob La Rosa, and my best redhead friend, Tom DeTrinis. Tom, in particular, really gave me an outlet to talk about redhead things in a way I never really could with anyone else. To quote *The Golden Girls*, thank you for being a friend, Tom.

Last but certainly not least, I need to thank my cat, Fish. While she admittedly reaped the benefits of me being home more while writing this book, she also spent countless hours curled up next to me and never complained when I typed too loudly or was flipping through reference books right next to her face. I just want to make you proud, Fish, and I hope I have.

PHOTO ACKNOWLEDGMENTS

Huge thanks for all the gorgeous emoji art throughout the book goes to EmojiOne, who supplied the art.

Major claps to FreeVectors.com, who supplied some of the graphics.

And a standing ovation for Pixabay and its users, for supplying us with some very cool images as well.

NOTES

1   David Robson, "How the Colour Red Warps the Mind," BBC (September 1, 2014), http://www.bbc.com/future/story/20140827-how-the-colour-red-warps-the-mind.

2   Marc Horne, "Expert Argues Vikings Carried Redhead Gene to Scotland," *Scotsman* (November 2013), http://www.scotsman.com/heritage/people-places/expert-argues-vikings-carried-redhead-gene-to-scotland-1-3200177.

3   "William II, Rufus the Red," *Britannia* (2013), http://www.britannia.com/history/monarchs/mon23.html.

4   Marion Roach, *The Roots of Desire*, Bloomsbury USA (2005), p. 82.

5   Jacky Colliss Harvey, *Red: A History of the Redhead*, Hachette Book Group (2015), p. 149.

6   Dianna Mazzone, "Tips to Prevent Your (Unnaturally) Red Hair from Fading," *InStyle* (April 22, 2015), http://www.instyle.com/news/tips-prevent-your-unnaturally-red-hair-fading.

7   Molly Mulshine, "Match.com Pushes Stats About Slutty Redheads in Honor of St. Patrick's Day," Yahoo (March 17, 2014), https://www.yahoo.com/news/match-com-pushes-stats-slutty-redheads-honor-st-205217794.html?ref=gs.

8   Carrie Anton, "The 4 Types of People Having the Most Orgasms," *Women's Health* (February 6, 2014), http://www.womenshealthmag.com/sex-and-love/more-orgasms.

9   Alex Kasprak and Kirsten King, "14 Myths About Sex That Need to Be Debunked Immediately," BuzzFeed (August 6, 2015), https://www.buzzfeed.com/alexkasprak/redheads-have-more-fun?utm_term=.gvYLQYN5wd#.kkWQ8lgker.

10 Lisette Mejia, "The Most Shocking Stats on Sex, Dating, and Relationships," PopSugar (January 28, 2015), http://www.popsugar.com/love/photo-gallery/34042728/image/34042730/Redheads-Orgasm-More.

11 Alanna Nuñez, "Match.com Releases 2014 Singles in America Results," *Shape*

http://www.shape.com/blogs/shape-your-life/matchcom-releases-2014-singles-america-results.

12 "'Hot' Redheads Bound for Extinction," UPI (August 3, 2004), http://www.upi.com/Odd_News/2004/08/03/Hot-redheads-bound-for-extinction/69981091556025/.

13 Patricia McNamee Rosenberg, "Requiem for the Redhead: The Next Great Extinction—Carrot Tops" *Smithsonian Magazine* (February 2009), http://www.smithsonianmag.com/arts-culture/requiem-for-the-redhead-44791525/?no-ist.

14 Robin L. Flanigan, "Will Rare Redheads Be Extinct by 2100?" *Seattle Times* (May 9, 2005), http://www.seattletimes.com/life/lifestyle/will-rare-redheads-be-extinct-by-2100/.

15 Cort Cass, *Redhead Handbook: A Fun and Comprehensive Guide to Red Hair and More*, Blue Mountain Arts (2003), p. 14.

16 Laura Bleakley, "Redheaded Donors Are Being Turned Away at Sperm Bank," BBC News (September 21, 2011), http://www.bbc.com/news/uk-northern-ireland-15001467.

17 Stephen W. Eldridge, "Ideological Incompatibility: The Forced Fusion of Nazism and Protestant Theology and Its Impact on Anti-Semitism in the Third Reich," *International Social Science Review*, vol. 81, no. 3/4 (2006), pp. 151–65.

18 "Bryce Dallas Howard Sings 'I Am Not Jessica Chastain' Song," *Hollywood Reporter* (June 9, 2015), http://www.hollywoodreporter.com/news/bryce-dallas-howard-sings-i-801342.

19 "'Ehu People: The Redheads of Polynesia," Hawaiian Time Machine. http://hawaiiantimemachine.blogspot.com/2012/08/ehu-people-redheads-of-polynesia.html.

20 Melissa Healy, "A Genetic Link Between Red Hair, Freckles and Skin Cancer," *Washington Post* (July 15, 2016), https://www.washingtonpost.com/national/health-science/why-redheads-and-their-children-seem-to-get-skin-cancer-more-than-others/2016/07/15/1be34fa2-487f-11e6-90a8-fb84201e0645_story.html.

21 Harvey, *Red*, p. 15.

22 Steve Bradt, "DNA Reveals Neanderthal Redheads," *Harvard Gazette* (November 1, 2007), http://news.harvard.edu/gazette/story/2007/11/dna-reveals-neanderthal-redheads/.

23 Melissa Hogenboom, "What Did the Neanderthals Do For Us?" BBC, (November 2015), http://www.bbc.com/earth/story/20151116-what-did-the-neanderthals-do-for-us.

24 Roach, *Roots of Desire*, p. 18.

25 John Boardman, *The Cambridge Ancient History*, vol. 3, part 1, Cambridge University Press (1970), p. 836.

26 Harvey, *Red*, p. 32.

27 Katie Kubesh, Niki McNeil, and Kimm Bellotto, *Mythological Creatures Around the World*, In the Hands of a Child (2007), p. 14.

28 Walter Gregor, "Some Scottish Folklore of the Child and the Human Body," *Folklore*, vol. 6, no. 4 (December 1895), pp. 394–97.

29 Roach, *Roots of Desire*, p. 49.

30 Harvey, *Red*, pp. 46–50.

31 Lowry Charles Wimberly, "The Red-Headed Man," *Prairie Schooner*, vol. 3, no. 4 (Fall 1929), pp. 284–90.

32 Harvey, *Red*, p. 71.

33 Roach, *Roots of Desire*, p. 72.

34 Margaret Donsbach, "Boudica: Celtic War Queen Who Challenged Rome," *Military History* (April 2004), http://www.historynet.com/boudica-celtic-war-queen-who-challenged-rome.htm.

35 Matthew Moore, "Facebook 'Kick a Ginger' Campaign Prompts Attacks on Redheads," *Telegraph* (November 22, 2008), http://www.telegraph.co.uk/news/worldnews/northamerica/canada/3498766/Facebook-Kick-a-Ginger-campaign-prompts-attacks-on-redheads.html.

36 Katherine Thompson, "Kids Attack Redheads on 'Kick a Ginger' Day," *Newser* (November 23, 2008), http://www.newser.com/story/43461/kids-attack-redheads-on-kick-a-ginger-day.html.

37 "Assault on Red-Haired Student Investigated as Hate Crime," CBC News (November 21, 2008), http://www.cbc.ca/news/canada/calgary/assault-on-red-haired-student-investigated-as-hate-crime-1.704812.

38 Sandy Banks, "'Kick a Ginger Day' Leaves a Bitter Lesson," *Los Angeles Times* (December 5, 2009), http://articles.latimes.com/2009/dec/05/local/la-me-banks5-2009dec05.

39 Anna Edwards, "Schoolchildren Beaten Up After Classmates Organise 'Kick a

Ginger Kid Day' Inspired by *South Park*," *Daily Mail* (October 18, 2013), http://www.dailymail.co.uk/news/article-2465752/Schoolchildren-beaten-classmates-organise-kick-ginger-kid-day-inspired-South-Park.html.

40 "Popular Teenager Killed Himself After Being 'Bullied' About His Ginger Hair, Inquest Hears," *Express* (November 14, 2013), http://www.express.co.uk/news/uk/443002/Popular-teenager-killed-himself-after-being-bullied-about-his-ginger-hair-inquest-hears.

41 Eleanor Harding, "Make Ginger Taunts a Hate Crime, Says Father of Girl, 15, Found Dead in the Woods After Being Bullied," *Daily Mail* (November 28, 2013), http://www.dailymail.co.uk/news/article-2514859/Helena-Farrell-15-killed-bullied-ginger.html.

42 Laura Clout, "Bullied for Being Ginger? Try Hair Dye," *Telegraph* (June 5, 2007), http://www.telegraph.co.uk/news/uknews/1553643/Bullied-for-being-ginger-Try-hair-dye.html.

INDEX

ABOUT THE AUTHOR

Author photo credit: Joanne Pio

ERIN LA ROSA is a writer living in Los Angeles. As a writer for BuzzFeed, she frequently writes about the perils and triumphs of being a redhead. Before BuzzFeed, Erin worked for the comedy Web sites Funny or Die and MadAtoms, as well as Wetpaint, Ecorazzi, and E!s *Fashion Police*. Erin has appeared on CNN, *Headline News*, *Jimmy Kimmel Live!*, and *Today* on behalf of BuzzFeed. You can follow her at @SideofGinger.